Fritz Spiegl's Book of
MUSICAL BLUNDERS
and other Musical Curiosities

Fritz Spiegl's Book of
MUSICAL BLUNDERS
and other
Musical Curiosities

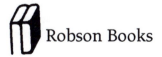
Robson Books

First published in Great Britain in 1996 by Robson Books Ltd,
Bolsover House, 5–6 Clipstone Street, London W1P 8LE

Copyright © 1996 Fritz Spiegl

The right of Fritz Spiegl to be identified as author of this
work has been asserted by him in accordance with the
Copyright, Design and Patents Act 1988

British Library Cataloguing in Publication Data
A catalogue record of this title is available from the British
Library
Book design by Harold King

ISBN 1 86105 075 5

Set in Berkeley by The Harrington Consultancy, London
Printed and bound in Great Britain by Butler & Tanner Ltd.,
Frome and London

Contents

For
Mark Cohen
(whose idea it was)
in admiration

Preface

I have overheard Continental musicians reminiscing together, and they seemed to concentrate on past triumphs – usually punctuating their stories with 'It vos a great success!'

British musicians with time to spare, in bandrooms and airport lounges, tend – contrarily – to recall not triumphs but disasters – blunders committed on the platform or in the opera house, usually with the words, 'Do you remember the time when . . . ?' There is more to musical blunders than wrong notes, 'dominoes', or conductors getting lost and taking the orchestra with them: therefore this book contains Musical Curiosities as well as Blunders.

In much of it I make a retrospective exhibition of myself – material originally used in BBC talks and music programmes, stuff that has piled up over the years – not so much researched as accidentally and serendipitously stumbled across. Some goes back to 'The Thud Programme' (as old-fashioned announcers called it), when I compiled some series of *Musical Curiosities* for veteran producers like David Cox, Julian Budden and Roger Fiske, for the BBC World Service as well as Radios 3 and 4. Some of this ephemeral material has now found a more permanent home here. More recent series were called *Serendipity*, *Diversions*, *An ABC of Musical Curios* (on TV as well as radio) and most of all, for a dozen years from the early 1980s, the nightly *Mainly for Pleasure*.

In spite of its illogical title ('What's the rest for – pain?' listeners asked) *Mainly for Pleasure* gave unrivalled opportunities to those who felt inclined to build structured (at first two-hour, latterly 90-minute) programmes that were more than mere successions of unrelated musical noises punctuated by a few friendly words (now alas the norm). What was particularly satisfying was that they enabled one to create topical music programmes while bypassing the customary channels: proposal, submission, discussion, planning (and possible rejection – the now ubiquitous words 'mission-statement' and 'strategy' had yet to enter BBC-speak); so that, for example, a British Museum exhibition of Fakes could be celebrated within days by a couple of *Mainly for Pleasures* of Musical Fakes, followed by one on Musical Blunders. The demise of *Punch* (now happily resuscitated) resulted in two music programmes celebrating the magazine's traditional preoccupation with music, musical snobbery and the musically ridiculous. By kind permission of the new proprietors and Mr Punch's librarian, Miranda Taylor, some of the wonderful drawings of George du Maurier, Raven Hill, Phil May etc are included.

Also reflected are several series of programmes compiled for Andrew Mussett, *Musical Times Past*, which encouraged many hours' browsing in old musical periodicals, which turned up curious old advertisements and advice from musical agony uncles; also the series *Words and Music*, for Ray Abbott – poetry and prose with and about music. To these I owe an introduction to (now alas the late) Virginia Graham and her deliciously witty verse. An anonymous listener sent several charming poems under the pseudonym 'Attacca', one of which appears here.

That type of programme came to an end with the new, accountant-led and finance-driven regime at the BBC, which replaced them with 'strands' of musical wallpaper in imitation of the successful Classic FM and its chat'n'plug 'shows'.

Numerous friends and colleagues, including Richard Adeney, Manfred Arlan, Robert Braga, the oboist James Brown, Christopher Driver, Prof Arthur Jacobs, Gareth Morris and Peter Spaull, often pointed me in the direction of stories and anecdotes – all carefully checked with that great purveyor of musical stories, Ben Trovato. Aviva Sklan in New York sought out newspaper archives about musicians' blunders against the law. The Abstracts from the Patent Office of silly inventions I owe to the late, lamented Bill Flood, brass teacher at a Liverpool school, who tried but failed to make a trumpeter out of young John Birt – a failure which indirectly proved a major musical calamity for the BBC. Michael K Jackson did some of the music typesetting. Kate Mills and Robson Books' editorial department patiently sifted stacks of material and selected and edited what appears here. Apart from the broadcasts and a few paragraphs in my – now out of print – *Music through the Looking Glass*, none of the material in this book has been previously anthologized. Few of the stories, oddly enough, came from conductor friends – about whom orchestral players tend to maintain a healthy scepticism. The baton is always in the key of C, never needs to transpose and cannot play wrong notes. If it beats the wrong number of beats in a bar, or gives a downbeat where there should be a sidebeat, the audience is usually none the wiser; except that next morning's papers will say that 'the players' ensemble was poor'. A story from the late Peter Beavan, long-service cellist in the Philharmonia Orchestra, confirms this happening during a concert conducted by the deified Arturo Toscanini. Some of the divergent critical opinions towards the end of the book were sent to me by Ernest Bean, the first general manager of the Royal Festival Hall.

1

The Conductor
or
The Composer's Best Friend

Gymnast of the podium
And darling of the crowd.
Oh, how the people *love* it
When the music's loud!

Never mind what Mahler wrote,
It's what *he* does that counts;
And so the sweat comes pouring out
And so the tension mounts.

A fat recording contract
Is safe beneath his belt;
He will record the works of X—,
For X amount of Geld.

And when the discs come slipping out,
The critics get to work –
Comparing his with Maestro B's,
A task they *never* shirk.

The columns of the music press
Are filled with loads of stuff
Re: tempi, balance and the like –
The going's really tough!

The *hoi polloi* all 'ooh!' and 'ah!'
As scribblers take no rest
They always buy the records that
The critics say are 'best'.

Our maestro now can live abroad,
And jet-set here and there;
Today in France, tomorrow, Spain –
His visits here are rare.

But hark! Amid the rush and fuss,
I think I hear a sound –
It is, I fear, old Mahler's corpse . . .
Rotating in the ground.

Attacca

Maestro and his keen ear

The acuity of conductors' ears is often – literally – legendary, for they hear things lesser mortals do not. One, anxious to impress the orchestra, pencilled a wrong note into the sixth double-bass part before the rehearsal, then, in a loud passage stopped the orchestra and said, 'Sixth double bass, you played a B flat!'

Double-bass: 'No, I played a B natural, but some bloody fool pencilled in a flat.'

Another maestro called out to a bassoonist: 'Mr Jones, you are playing an F sharp. Should be F natural.'

Bassoonist: 'It was an F natural when it left here.'

Sir Georg Solti, whose keen ear belies his advancing years, stopped the Covent Garden Orchestra during rehearsal and asked the principal trumpet: 'Vot make is your instrument?'

The trumpeter told him it was by Boosey and Hawkes.

Solti replied: 'You should try a Besson. Moch, moch bettair tone.'

Later in the rehearsal another player raised his hand as if to ask about a point of interpretation: 'Excuse me, Sir Georg.'

Solti: 'Yes, vot is it?'

Player: 'Sir Georg, what make is your baton?'

Erich Leinsdorf is quite a nice chap

The conductor Erich Leinsdorf (1912-1993) was much feared by orchestral players – insofar as orchestral players are any longer afraid of conductors: they realize that *they* make the sound, whereas the conductor's baton is silent. But unpleasantness makes for uncomfortable rehearsals, and Leinsdorf's reputation as a tyrant went before him. For the first half-hour of his first rehearsal with the London Philharmonic there was a subdued atmosphere and all went smoothly. Then a back-desk viola player whispered to his partner out of the corner of his mouth, 'He seems to be quite a nice chap, really.' Leinsdorf screamed, 'Kviet down zere!'

Sir Malcolm Sargent's natural talents

Sir Malcolm Sargent's natural talents were probably wasted when he decided to become a conductor. He achieved renown and a modest fortune but had he put his mind to it, or more likely if he had enjoyed the right family connections, his quicksilver mind, clarity in presenting an argument (he was nearly always right and knew it) would have taken him to the top of any profession, the diplomatic service or the law. He might have been a natural lord chancellor and perhaps even prime minister, just as the Polish pianist Paderewski (with little or no political experience) was invited to be the first prime minister of his country. But Sargent came from a humble background. His father was a coal merchant in Stamford, Lincolnshire, who acted as organist and choirmaster for his local church in his spare time. This is how the young Malcolm's interest in music was awakened. It is probably fair to say that he was not a 'natural' musician, either as a pianist or conductor, but a hard-working one who seldom made a mistake. In his rather aloof manner he was charming to players socially and was not above telling them slightly risqué stories. I can personally attest to his kindness to young and inexperienced players, to whom he always gave confidence on the platform.*

* A personal footnote: my parents and I had been separated during the war; and after I had been safely dispatched to England they were able to flee to South America. When Sargent conducted there he went to see them – he did not summon them but took a taxi to find them.

4

While rehearsing a Strauss waltz with the BBC Symphony Orchestra (some of whose players thought him overbearing and were sometimes openly hostile to him), Sir Malcolm heard a player remark, not sufficiently under his breath, 'Too fast.' Sargent said, 'What do you mean "too *fast*"? Only last night I was dancing a waltz with the Queen Mother.' As if that gave him a direct line to the Waltz King himself.

Part of an obituary interview,
October 1967,
BBC Radio News

The curtain and the evening dress

The poet Samuel Taylor Coleridge is sometimes confused with the English composer, Samuel Coleridge-Taylor (1875-1912). The latter was of Sierra Leone descent and proudly described himself as being 'half African'. His daughter Gwendolen (born in 1903) followed in her father's footsteps, though chiefly as a conductor, changing her first name to Avril for the purpose, while using other pseudonyms as a composer. I played under her when I was a student on, I think, the stage of the Scala Theatre in London. On such occasions it was customary for orchestras to assemble on stage while the curtain was still down, to be revealed fully ready to play (or indeed, with a flourish, already playing). Miss Coleridge-Taylor was standing on the rostrum, baton raised. As the curtain rose, part of it became tangled with the hem of her long evening dress – which it slowly but relentlessly pulled over her head.

Barbirolli's concern

Barbirolli was almost obsessionally concerned about the welfare of his musicians. When, on a foreign tour, there was confusion about hotel bookings and it seemed for a time as if some players would be without a bed, he insisted they were all accommodated before he accepted a room for himself.

The Hallé had at that time a reputation for containing the largest number of illicit couples of any British orchestra, though there was a constantly changing counterpoint of liaisons. The permissive society was then not far enough advanced for couples to share rooms openly, so they would collude, pair by pair, two men and two women officially sharing as room-mates, but one man and one woman changing beds unofficially.

When the tour was over and the plane landed at Manchester airport, the husbands would run into the arms of wives and children, while the single girls would creep away to their cold bedsitters.

There were always domestic and emotional dramas (with the occasional mischief-maker informing on some liaison) and when one wife found out about her husband's longstanding affair with a female member of the orchestra, she told her woes to Barbirolli.

He was sympathetic, gave her a comforting hug and patted her on the shoulder. 'There, there,' he said, 'it'll all come right I tell you – it'll just blow over.' Then he added, brightly, as an afterthought, 'And besides, he's playing better than ever.'

The wing commander wings Beethoven

During the Second World War many of the top London musicians, who had been conscripted for the duration, joined the Central

Band of the Royal Air Force. They included the horn player Dennis Brain and his oboist brother Leonard, the flautist Gareth Morris, the entire Griller String Quartet, the violinist Frederick Grinke and numerous other distinguished young performers (most of whom later reappeared in the newly founded Philharmonia Orchestra). The blue uniforms of the RAF were a familiar sight on the London concert platforms, especially at the daily lunchtime concerts at the National Gallery, although some of the musicians were sometimes less than perfectly turned out. Naturally the reluctant bandsmen wanted to play 'real' music as well as marches, so the band occasionally gave symphony concerts under its conductor, Wing Commander O'Donnell. He was a little out of his depth in the classical repertoire, and one day Aircraftsman

MODEST APPEAL

Lady (to big drum): PRAY, MY GOOD MAN, DON'T MAKE THAT HORRID NOISE! I CAN'T HEAR MYSELF SPEAK.

(By kind permission of *Punch*)
1868

Frederick Grinke was to play the Beethoven Violin Concerto. O'Donnell clearly had not studied the score (let alone recordings of the work) and began the first movement under the impression that it started with the oboes and bassoons in the second bar – having failed to spot the opening four solo timpani notes, whose rhythm pervades the whole of the first movement. He brought down his stick for the oboes but instead, the timpanist went 'bom-bom-bom-bom' just as Beethoven indicated. On hearing the drumbeats he rapped on his desk and called to the timpanist, 'Thank you very much, but I don't need *you* to give me the tempo.'

The drummer fears Paganini

Professor Ella, that Nestor of critics, to whom England owes so much as the father of chamber-music concerts, once told Joachim that when he was playing amongst the violins at one of Paganini's rehearsals, the drummer got so alarmed in the presence of the virtuoso that he trembled almost too much to hold his drumsticks; and Ella, laying down his violin, went to the drums and took his place, receiving the thanks of Paganini, who was fast losing his patience with the nervous drummer. Still, drummers who have been abused are not always to blame. We have all heard of the ignorant manager-proprietor who, being present at an orchestra rehearsal, observed that the drummer did next to nothing, and went up to him to expostulate. 'But sir,' says the drummer, 'I'm resting – don't you see?' and he pointed to his part. 'Damme, sir,' says the manager, 'I do not pay you to rest; I pay you to play.'

The Violin Times
May 1897

Signor Toscanini remembers – and forgets

Toscanini was the first modern conductor with a publicity machine behind him issuing slanted press releases that added to the carefully fostered mystique of a man who supposedly possessed superhuman powers. That is probably how the anecdotes arose about his phenomenal memory which are still being repeated – and embroidered – to this day.

Thus Anthony Burgess in the *Spectator* (10 July 1982), 'A double-bass player, whose E string had broken, asked in the interval, to be excused playing in the rest of the concert ... Toscanini thought for a moment and then said, "You can play. You don't use the E string in this half."' Piffle. It would be a rum kind of band whose entire bass section was unable to muster a spare E string between them; and an even rummer concert in which all the music played in the whole of the second half never ventured below A, avoiding the E string of the bass altogether, the very fundament of the string sound so dear to Toscanini. Burgess himself claimed to be a composer, so one wonders what his orchestration was like.

Most musical anecdotes accrete barnacles, especially when told and retold by people unfamiliar with the subject. A slightly more plausible – though still absurd – version of Burgess's story is allegedly about Toscanini's bass clarinettist. 'Maestro,' he is supposed to have said, 'I cannot play tonight. My E flat key has broken off.' Maestro closed his eyes, knitted his brow in the conductors' favourite I-am-concentrating gesture (you often see it just before the start of a work: they bow their heads and grasp the ridges of their noses with the first two fingers like a pince-nez). We are encouraged to believe that the entire score flashed before Toscanini in a couple of seconds, like the life of a drowning man. After a moment or two he looked up and said, 'Yes, my friend, you *can* play. That note does not appear in your part.'

If this story *is* true and the incident with the bass clarinettist actually occurred, it indeed illustrates Toscanini's prodigious memory, of which there was no doubt. But it also reveals a crass ignorance of how wind instruments work. Did he think that to play a note on a bass clarinet one blew down it, while at the same time – as on a piano – simply pressing the required key? In reality, a single broken key on any wind instrument puts almost the entire instrument out of action. The bass clarinettist's reply to Maestro is not recorded but his private thoughts would have been interesting.

The story always put about was that Toscanini's eyesight was so poor that as an orchestral player he had to memorize his part. More piffle. The essence of orchestral playing is reading, often sight-reading, and watching while playing and listening. The player who needs advance notice of what is to be played ('I'll take it home and learn it') is all but useless even in an amateur orchestra: blind people play chess, football and have climbed Everest, but I know of no blind orchestral musician. Besides, Toscanini's eyesight was remarkably good when there was a pretty woman to be seen.

Feats of memory were not unique to him. The cellist Peter Beavan, in his book, *Philharmonia Days*, says that Lorin Maazel also had a 'fantastic memory and impeccable stick technique. If Arthur Wilson asked about a trombone note he would instantly recite and sing the notes of the whole brass section; and with how many other conductors could you look up and actually see what beat you were supposed to be playing?'

Many people still consider Toscanini the greatest conductor of the twentieth century, while others say he was the most over-rated and over-hyped in recent history. Some have described his rigid beat as musical butchery, especially when compared to the more human approach of contemporaries like Bruno Walter and Otto Klemperer. In his last years Toscanini mellowed and became less rigid and metronomic in his conducting – and less bad-tempered. Even his famous memory occasionally failed him. As Peter Beavan recalled:

We had Toscanini for two memorable Brahms concerts. He had got past the fiery intensity of earlier days and his music flowed naturally just as it did later with Klemperer. There was time to turn corners without in any way losing the overall rhythm. They had a special ramp built for him so that he could, at 85, walk to the rostrum unaided. The first concert, however, started like a nightmare: with a packed and expectant audience and a super-tense atmosphere we commenced with the *Tragic Overture* [by Brahms]. To our horror Toscanini gave a succession of quick, powerful beats. We rocked until Jim Merrett [double-bass] and Raymond Clark [cello] took it unto themselves to play the opening bass theme 'fortissimo'. Toscanini recovered himself and all went well. Afterwards he told Manoug Parikian, then our leader, that he'd forgotten we were to start with the *Tragic* and was concentrating on the First Symphony. No one outside seemed aware of it but for us it was shattering.

At Toscanini's last appearance at the Salzburg Festival in 1937 he conducted Verdi's *Falstaff* but the performances almost failed to materialize because of his temper, which an artist should surely be able to control, along with speeds and dynamics, however temperamental he may be. Many a potentially good orchestral performance has been ruined by tyrannical conductors, just as road-rage makes for bad driving.

Toscanini was almost like a sadist in that he seemed to enjoy humiliating not only the orchestral players but also fellow artists of international standing. During *Falstaff* rehearsals in Salzburg he threw the score at four different women soloists on four different occasions, alleging that they had not learnt it. He also assaulted a timpanist, who wisely defended himself with fisticuffs; but the conductor also kicked out at and dented one of his drums. The orchestra, quite rightly, went on strike. They agreed to play for him only after getting a grovelling apology. He said, 'Forgive me, I only do it for Verdi.' He was lying. He did it for Toscanini. Either he suffered from some personality disorder and could not help it; or, more likely, he wanted to foster the myth that had grown around him of a man who cared for no one's feelings, nor of what people thought of him, only about musical truth.

In one of his tantrums he tore his gold watch from its chain, flung it to the floor and stamped on it. His musicians watched with nervous amusement. Before the next rehearsal they clubbed together, bought a cheap nickel watch and had it inscribed 'For Maestro – for Rehearsal Purposes Only'. They left it on his desk, so that he would find it when he arrived. No one would have dared answer back.

During a rehearsal with the Vienna Philharmonic Toscanini threw one of his expected tantrums, without at least one of which no rehearsal was complete. He lifted his heavy score as high as he could with both hands and, cursing and swearing at the orchestra in obscene Italian, crashed it down on the floor. The principal cellist, Friedrich Buxbaum, whose quiet, ironic humour is still a legend in Vienna, rose from his seat and calmly placed his cello part on top of Toscanini's score.

Even a well-meant gesture by a concert promoter was spoilt by Toscanini's disregard for other people's feelings. In the late 1930s he opened a series of subscription concerts in Prague with the Vienna Philharmonic. He was given the red-carpet treatment literally: as a mark of respect, a red carpet was procured and unrolled from the stage-left entrance to the podium. A player recalled that the concert was about to start, with everyone seated on the platform, but Toscanini refused to enter. Instead some stagehands appeared and removed it. *'Non sono un cardinale!'* he growled, 'I'm not a cardinal.'

The most meaningful words of praise orchestral players can find for a conductor are 'He lets us play'. Toscanini did not. Recordings taken at his rehearsals show that he was constantly tapping on the desk to stop the orchestra, as other conductors do; but he also kept screaming – there is no other word for it – 'No – NO – NO-O-O!' in a crescendo of exasperation, sometimes adding a few well-chosen obscenities (his orchestras were all male, with the possible exception of the harpist, a kind of honorary man). His players used to call him 'Toscanono', though not to his face.

Most of the adulatory stories, generated by his publicity machine, were dutifully repeated by the press, and probably embellished. *The Musical Times*, however, used to deflating pompous politicians, refused to be hoodwinked and, on 1 October 1920, exposed some of the stories surrounding the conductor as crude (and, as they delighted in pointing out, ill-written) publicity stunts.

Feet of clay

Toscanini myths continue to circulate today and, while his recordings have all been remastered on CD, his interpretations often sound curiously crude, so that his stock has fallen in recent decades while Beecham's has risen. Today's orchestral players, backed by their unions, have ways of bringing the most authoritarian conductors down to earth and revealing feet of clay; and players are now less likely to be sacked for insubordination. The violinist Peter Gibson, a distinguished Second World War veteran (who often flew to concerts in his light aeroplane and eventually lost his life in it) one day decided he had had enough of Herbert von Karajan's imperious manner. He said quietly, 'I spent five years fighting Nazi bastards like you and I'm not taking any more' and walked off the platform.

No trifles please

The London Chamber Orchestra was rehearsing for a live BBC broadcast. Things had not gone well and as usual time ran out. As the studio manager's voice came over the loudspeakers, 'Stand by for a light in ten seconds from now' and the conductor, Anthony

"Very goot! Very goot!!"

AN ORCHESTRAL REHEARSAL.

"Are you ready, Shentlemen?"

AN ORCHESTRAL REHEARSAL.

Come along please!

"You 2nd Fiddles! Vill you please make zat pizzicato more marked?"

AN ORCHESTRAL REHEARSAL.

Bernard, raised his baton, the leader asked, 'Mr Bernard, what's the order?' Bernard hissed back, 'Don't bother me with trifles!'

To the gentleman in row E

Dear Sir, we in Row E are well aware
Your soul is steeped in music to the core.
You love, we notice, each succeeding air
More deeply than the one which came before.

You lead the orchestra in perfect time
With ever-nodding head you set the pace,
We in Row E consider it a crime
You are not in Sir Thomas Beecham's place.

Your lily hands most delicately haver
Each phrase is ended with a graceful twist,
You know, it seems, each breve and semi-quaver,
And play them gently on your other wrist.

Sometimes you hum the least familiar portions,
And beat upon the floor a faint tattoo,
Though we can stand a lot of your contortions,
We shouldn't tap too much if I were you!

Dear Sir, we need no musical instructor,
We also sang in oratorio,
And if you were a really good conductor,
Our lightning would have struck you hours ago!

Consider the Years, Virginia Graham, 1946

Reginald Goodall loves all things German – including Adolf Hitler

To say that the conductor Sir Reginald Goodall was a Germanophile is an understatement. He was a fervent and unreconstructed admirer of everything Teutonic, not excluding the Third Reich and Adolf Hitler – and it all stemmed from the fact that he worshipped Hitler's hero Richard Wagner.

The fact that Goodall achieved public recognition only late in life may have been partly the result of his naive political views (which he propounded to anyone who would listen) but mostly because he was not actually a terribly good conductor. However, even the worst and most boring ones eventually improve with age: provided they can still mount the rostrum and wave their arms about, their readings will eventually come to be described as 'authoritative', which usually earns them the standard-issue knighthood for long-service conductors. The history of English music is littered with knights – especially Victorian and Edwardian – who within a couple of decades of their death had sunk without trace.

Goodall in fact owed his late summer largely to a persistent campaign by two London music critics, whose joint views never coincided with those of their colleagues, still less the views of the orchestral players who had to endure his presence on the rostrum and singers his snail-like tempi when he was a *répétiteur*.

Karl Böhm – another Nazi, as it happens, but one who had the sense to keep quiet after 1945 – mellowed wonderfully towards the end of his life. Goodall, however, took this slowing down to an absurd degree of exaggeration, and his Ring, admired by some, was declared almost sclerotic by others. Besides, by the time success overtook him, Goodall was as deaf as a post and barely able to hear what his players said to him.

The musical blunder for which he will always be remembered was to conduct Wagner's Ring cycle more slowly than anyone else.

Rehearsals as well as performances always produced mutterings of discontent from the pit ('Hasn't he got a home to go to?') as every performance became like a 'slow bicycle race'. Progressive slowing up, or down, during the course of a work is one of the marks of the bad conductor (just as a progressive drop in pitch is the mark of an untrained unaccompanied choir). Such conductors do not lead the orchestra but merely 'ride' on its sound. The conductor waits for the sound and the players wait for the beat; so eventually the music practically stops.

Goodall's support for Nazi Germany throughout the war was considered treasonable by those who knew of it, and he narrowly escaped internment as a potential fifth columnist; but his praise for Hitler proves that Goodall was probably a little unhinged. He railed against successive Continental conductors at Covent Garden, refugees from Nazism to whom, as a long-serving humble *répétiteur*, he was obliged to kow-tow: first Karl Rankl and then Sir Georg Solti.

At the height of the Second World War an appalling incident occurred which sent shudders through the profession. On a railway platform, while Goodall and the Wessex Symphony Orchestra, a morale-boosting wartime combination he conducted for a time, were waiting for a train, his suitcase burst open. This is embarrassing for anyone at the best of times, but among Goodall's soiled socks and shirts and scores that fell out was something far dirtier – Nazi propaganda publications, which were picked up for him by helpful orchestra members. Several of these later attested to this event, and among them was a young freelance trumpeter who later became the composer Sir Malcolm Arnold.

Goodall spoke German fluently but must have learnt it from books – or else here, too, demonstrated that he had cloth ears. For he persisted in pronouncing German words as if they were English: *Vorspiel und Liebestod* came out as 'War-spile and Lye-bee-shtodd'. But then, many conductors are unblessed with powers of mimicking foreign accents – a question of having good ears. Few can sing, and we have all heard those who, after spending half a century or more among English-speaking people in Britain or the United States, still insist, conversely, on pronouncing English as if it were German.

The commissars do not like conductors

Both the idea and the acronym might have come out of Orwell's *Animal Farm*. 'Persimfans' stood for '*Pervyi Simfonichesky Ansambl*' and was one of the looniest of loony-left inventions – the Soviet conductorless orchestra. This was formed in 1922 in an attempt to apply to music the principles of Socialist equality (a sham, as the Supreme Conductor Lenin had a chauffeur-driven Rolls-Royce). The culture commissars decided that the symphony orchestra was a western-style reactionary bourgeois assembly (or 'assambl'?) in which worker-musicians were subjugated into hireling running-dog lackeys by a single, power-wielding capitalist imperialist hyena who took undemocratic decisions without consulting the comrades on the shop floor. So the conductor was liquidated, and the orchestra run like a collective farm. Each freedom-loving worker-comrade would have an equal say at rehearsals, and instead of just playing the notes would gain a full dialectical awareness of every semiquaver.

What happened was that rehearsals turned into committee meetings ('Comrade principal bassoon, may I suggest your bottom B flat has a certain revisionist, counter-revolutionary loudness, a quality incompatible with the D on my tuba ...?') and music-making took ten times as long. The commissars soon discovered that an orchestra with 75 conductors was infinitely less efficient than it had been under a single one. In any case the 'leader' ('concert master') – that curious anachronism and double misnomer – filled the same role as in capitalist orchestras only more so. In no time things turned full circle, just as they did in

Animal Farm, when the pigs found that there was really quite a lot to be said for walking on two legs after all.

After ten years of 'workers' struggle' the experiment was quietly dropped. Prokofiev said of Persimfans that 'its principal difficulty lay in changing tempo', which just about summed up the entire Communist system – and led to its collapse.

This does not mean that conductorless orchestras are impracticable: far from it. But they do have certain limitations, like the lack of 'corporate phrasing', which is the only undisputed quality of a conductor and what he does best: most experienced orchestral players do not need a person to beat time for them, especially in baroque and classical works, where there would have been no conductor anyway.

Vain conductors

The celebrated March King, John Philip Sousa (1854-1932), was something of a practical joker. On one occasion he shaved off his beard and moustache during the interval of a concert and returned to the rostrum clean-shaven for the second half. This would never have occurred to Sir Thomas Beecham, who could have shed his moustache and goatee at half-time; or to Sir André Previn, who might have had his famous Beatle-style hair trimmed like a grown-up's (it eventually did disappear but long after the Beatles cut theirs). Conversely, the late Sir John Pritchard might have re-emerged on the platform without the 'rug' hairpiece he wore for most of his life to cover increasing baldness. He must be the only conductor to have been observed combing his hair while conducting Beethoven's 'Eroica'. Even Sir Malcolm Sargent resorted to a little black hair dye, cleverly letting his temples go gradually grey.

Pierre Monteux, on the other hand, allowed his luxuriant, bushy moustache to turn naturally white but blatantly dyed his head hair a jet black so uniform that it could only have been achieved with shoe polish. A colleague asked, in feigned innocence, 'Maestro, why is it that your hair is still black, whereas your moustache has gone white?'

Monteux replied, with the kind of naughty twinkle elderly Frenchmen are good at, 'Becoz se 'air on my 'ead 'az not 'ad ze same experi-awnces.' On another occasion, asked about his *joie de vivre*, he answered, with a shrug of his shoulders and a pun on Rimsky-Korsakov's opera, '*Le coq d'or.*'

More about Sousa

A musicologist, misled perhaps by a waggish informant, claimed that Sousa was of Japanese extraction, family name So, to which he added the letters USA upon naturalization. If you believe that, you must also believe the claim once put forward in a Liverpool paper that Donizetti was a Scouse Liverpudlian, born Donald Izett, who Italianized his former name. His opera *Emilia di Liverpool*, however, could hardly be used as evidence of Donizetti's familiarity with the city.

Sir Herbert Beerbohm Tree cuts Beethoven down to size

Theatrical actor-managers at the beginning of this century appear to have had little knowledge of music and even less sympathy for musicians. Sir Herbert Beerbohm Tree (1852-1907) was a greatly respected London 'manager-proprietor', as they were called. He was active when every theatre had a band, when musicians were still cheap and no one had yet dreamed of recorded incidental music. Tree had no idea of the work that might be involved in setting up a musical performance – for example, that orchestral players needed parts to play from. Incidental music, he thought, could simply be conjured up instantly, to provide his productions with atmospheric background. When he kept demanding last-minute changes in some piece of music specially written for him by Sir Hubert Parry, the composer, clearly unable to write an entire new score *and* copy out orchestral parts within the available hour, exploded: 'Look here, Tree, what you ought to do is go out into the street and hire a damned barrel organ.'

The Musical Times reported in 1909 that Tree had produced a play called *Beethoven* by René Fauchois, translated into English by Louis N Parker. This was based on incidents in the composer's life and made modest use of some of his music – the 'Moonlight' Sonata and such pieces. The conductor in His Majesty's Theatre, London, was the young Mr (later Sir) Landon Ronald, who presided over a tiny theatre band of about a dozen musicians. At the final dress rehearsal Tree suddenly had an idea. He leaned down into the pit and called to the conductor, 'Landon, when Beethoven dies in the last act, as the curtain drops, I want you to play the Ninth Symphony.'

According to the notice which subsequently appeared in *Punch*, Tree evidently had his way and Landon Ronald must somehow have been able to send out for the material of the Ninth. The magazine sent no mere drama critic: its editor, Owen Seaman himself, went along to the first performance. It was a mark of respect – one distinguished man reporting on the work of another (Seaman was himself knighted and was later still made a Baronet – Victorians honoured even the satirists). Seaman, however, could not resist poking fun at the misguided enterprise. He wrote in his report (1 December 1909): 'It would be easy enough to make merry over the latest of Sir Herbert Tree's sporting experiments, but a much harder matter to appraise it seriously ...'; and went on to complain about:

SYMPHONIES COMPOSED WHILE YOU WAIT
BEETHOVEN – SIR HERBERT TREE.

(By kind permission of *Punch*)
1909

The risky device of presenting the Master in the throes of composition – always a spectacle that comes perilously near to the ludicrous – with the orchestra taking it down bar by bar ... The Third Act, in which we saw the dying of Beethoven, was almost an anticlimax. It was eked out with certain painful family details, which somehow seemed to miss their ironical purpose, and rather detracted from the dignity of the scene. Nor did I care very greatly for ... a passage from the 'Ode to Joy' which followed immediately upon the musician's death, and seemed rather untimely in its gladness ... The orchestra, under the clever conduct of Mr Landon Ronald, was perhaps the best feature of the evening. I am not sure that we would not have had a better time if the music had gone on all the while. Sir Herbert, disguised as the Master, might have conducted.

Had he done so he would merely have added to the merriment of any musician present because, as everyone knows, actors cannot conduct (though many conductors can act – at being conductors). They wave their arms about in symmetrical contrary motion, approximately in time to the music, and usually behind it. Which is strange, as in the words of Sir Adrian Boult, 'Conducting is the only job that can be learnt in an evening.'

Lilac time

During the first half of the twentieth century, the rising cost of hiring living composers to write music for plays and films started a rush of dramas – from plays to musicals, films and even operas – in which the composer appears as the hero. He can then be accompanied by his own music, free of copyright fees (and it may be noticed that such productions are often carefully timed to appear just after a copyright has expired).

According to those who know about Norway and Grieg, the musical *Song of Norway* does an injustice to both the country and its most famous composer, having been cobbled together from large chunks of his Piano Concerto in A minor, his song 'Ich liebe Dich' and bits from the music for *Peer Gynt*. The plot, based loosely on a lurid exaggeration of the composer's alleged love life, bears no examination. This did not prevent its first run from 1944 from enjoying some 860 performances: there is no end to the market for sentimental bilge.

Schumann was romanticized in 1917 in an operetta called *Fahrende Musikanten* (Travelling Musicians) and a year later Liszt, his music and his mistresses figured in *Der Zigeuner* (The Gypsy).

Then it was Mendelssohn's turn, in 1920, with *Dichterliebe* (A Poet's Love – surely more suitable for Schumann, who composed a song of that name). Much of this nonsense was produced in Vienna, the birthplace of operetta, before taking off for the United States, away from the threat of Nazism, where it turned into the All-American musical, often with the same Viennese writers, arrangers and composers.

Tchaikovsky and his music produced no fewer than four operettas (none so much as hinting at his homosexuality): *Die Siegerin* (The Victress) in 1922, *Catherine* in 1923, *Nadja* in 1925 and *Music in My Heart* in 1947. Dvorak's story and his music featured in *Summer Song*, while Chopin was maligned in what is probably a record number of musicals, films and films-of-musicals, including *White Lilacs*, *Polonaise*, and *Waltz without End*.

Chopin also unwittingly – not to say prenatally – contributed the music to George Clutsam's *The Damask Rose*. Its action takes place in 1764, half a century before Chopin's birth – so much for authentic musical style. Clutsam was a music critic working for the London *Observer* from 1908 to 1918, but left after he made his first fortune with *Lilac Time*, courtesy of Franz Schubert, who was then nearly a hundred years dead. It was an adaptation of an adaptation of an adaptation, for it began life as an Austrian novel about Schubert's love life by Dr R H Bartsch, called *Schwammerl* (Little Mushroom – Schubert's nickname, because he was short, with a big head). In 1916, *Schwammerl* was turned into *Hannerl* (the name of one of the three female characters) and then *Das Dreimäderlhaus* (The Three Girls' House). It was at this point that it was brought across the Channel, fitted with an English translation by Clutsam and renamed *Lilac Time* (confusingly, the Americans insisted on calling it *Blossom Time*). Where Schubert's music could not be convincingly cannibalized, Clutsam composed extra bits of his own.

Among the hit songs of the show was Clutsam's adaptation of 'Hark! hark! the lark at Heaven's gate sings', to which he added a second verse:

Look, look, the cook
Has done his best
To bring the supper in.
Behold, the sausage
Swells his breast,
And almost bursts his skin,
He laughs to burst his skin!

Mendelssohn tests the conductors

An excellent way of testing a conductor is to find out whether he
has a good sense of pitch. The upper woodwind (flutes and oboes)
conspire to transpose the opening notes of Mendelssohn's
Midsummer Night's Dream overture by a semitone – up or down, it
doesn't matter. If he has absolute pitch he will notice at once. If he
has not he will get the shock of his life when the strings enter with
the correct notes. There will, however, be some strange looks from
the strings right from the beginning – as strings more often have
perfect pitch than do conductors.

The conductor's ear

Sir Thomas Beecham at rehearsal: Second trumpet – you're too loud.
    Leader, embarrassed: I'm sorry, Sir Thomas, but the second
trumpet phoned to say he would be a little late.
    Beecham, totally unembarrassed: Well, when he arrives tell him
he's too loud.
    This much-related story is in keeping with Beecham's quick wit
and gently barbed repartee.
    For what conductors hear and claim to hear are often two

different things. One maestro, keen to show off the acuity of his ear, got hold of a double-bass part before the rehearsal and altered one note. Then, at rehearsal, he stopped the orchestra: 'Fourth double-bass, you played an F sharp.' The player said, 'No, some bloody fool pencilled in an F sharp. I played an F natural as printed.'

Making do

Before Hugo Rignold became chief conductor of the Liverpool Philharmonic Orchestra in 1948 he spent some of his war service in Cairo, conducting the Middle East Symphony Orchestra. It was an ad hoc body, consisting of army musicians reinforced with such local or expatriate players as they could pick up and they travelled from army base to army base to entertain the troops, with never any time for rehearsals.

Rignold told me that on one occasion the orchestra assembled on the makeshift platform for a performance of Tchaikovsky's Piano Concerto No 1 (the great concerto hit during the war years and beyond). Rignold and the soloist, Eileen Joyce, walked on and the pianist sat down as the orchestra started the introduction. She open-ed the piano lid and and found that it had no keyboard. The furniture removers who brought the piano had forgotten to replace it.

Gresham's law of musical performance

The Anglo-Russian conductor Albert Coates made some historic recordings of Russian music with the London Symphony Orchestra between 1928 and 1932 (at any rate they are historic now, as they have been reissued on compact disc). In spite of his English name and parentage, Coates was essentially Russian, with a fiery Russian temperament, born in St Petersburg in 1882 but educated at Liverpool University. His conducting of Russian music is doubtless authentic; but he was also a pioneer of the excessively fast tempo now customary for Glinka's *Ruslan and Ludmilla* overture. His recordings show that he played this at such a fast speed that the semiquavers sound an unholy scramble and the syncopated offbeats tread on the heels of the main beat, as indeed they invariably now do in modern performances.

Ruslan is one of several works that have been irrevocably spoilt for the world by speed merchants: once a too-fast speed becomes established, other performers dare not opt for moderation for fear of sounding plodding or boring. Yet the very same tune which Glinka uses in the opening of the overture also occurs as the final chorus for the whole company at the end of the opera, where it

AGGRAVATING FLIPPANCY

Enthusiastic amateur: OH, HANG IT CELIA! NOT READY YET? AND I'VE GOT TO PLAY IN THE FIRST QUARTET ... *DO* LOOK SHARP!

Celia: NOW *DON'T* FIDGET, MY DEAR! THERE'S LOTS OF TIME AND, IF WE ARE A LITTLE LATE, YOU CAN PLAY A LITTLE FASTER, YOU KNOW ...

(By kind permission of *Punch*)

1870

must be (and is) taken at a singable speed, else the whole thing makes nonsense. It is the Gresham's law of musical performance: Bad tempi drive out good.

Another remarkable example is Mozart's *Marriage of Figaro* overture. Although marked 'presto' it is written in common time – not 'alla breve' or two-in-a-bar, but a nominal four beats; although no one would possibly now beat (or even think) it in four it is unlikely that in Mozart's day the overture would (or could) have been played at such absurd speeds. In my own experience of playing in live performances of this overture only Efrem Kurtz, another Russian conductor, had the courage to moderate the tempo: and although players at first looked at each other in disbelief, his interpretation proved a real ear-opener. With a 25 per cent reduction in pace one can actually *hear* Mozart's suspensions deliciously grating, for which other conductors never allow enough time. The Champagne aria in *Don Giovanni* is another victim: singers can seldom articulate their words and ruin the flow of the music as they gasp for a breath. Beethoven's Rondo a Capriccio Op 129 ('Rage over the lost penny') is the pianist's traditional speed blunder. The work is always played about twice its proper pace: the composer marked it not 'presto' but 'allegro vivace'; and in *two*-four, not one-in-a-bar. When played properly it is immediately recognizable as a typical Hungarian rondo. It was Artur Schnabel who popularized the hectic pace in the first decades of this century, after which other pianists followed his bad example. Since then none has dared play the rondo as it unquestionably should be played, just in case audiences might think they cannot play it fast.

Such worries did not concern the eccentric but wise Glenn Gould (1932-82), who played the Alla Turca of Mozart's A major Sonata K331 at a real allegretto pace as marked by Mozart, and makes it sound perfectly poised. At the first hearing it comes as something of a shock but, after a bar or two, one can almost hear the Turkish drums Mozart so cleverly characterized. Afterwards, all other versions sound too fast.

But, to return to Albert Coates; over-fast tempi were on at least one occasion a weapon for him to use against a rebellious orchestra. During the mid-1940s he directed the Liverpool Philharmonic Orchestra in Llandudno, with his wife, a singer, appearing as the principal soloist in both halves of the concert. The seaside audience loved her and demanded encore after encore, even before the interval. This, naturally, did not please the orchestra, who quietly reminded Coates during the break that they faced a long, late and uncomfortable coach journey home and would not be prepared to play so many encores in the second half. Coates agreed in bad grace and in such a black mood that he conducted the last work, Beethoven's Fifth Symphony, at such an insane speed that it made a mockery of the work. Even the slow movement was taken 'allegro', and the Scherzo became unplayable; he did not even give the players time to turn the pages or put their instruments down between movements. Many members of the audience walked out and Coates never conducted the orchestra again.

Blunders – musical and political

During a rehearsal with the Royal Liverpool Philharmonic Orchestra, the German conductor and teacher of conductors, Hermann Scherchen (1891-1966), berated the second horn player for some imperfection. The poor man was rather puzzled by the conductor's anger, as he had nothing to play at that point and knew perfectly well that the note in question in fact occurred in the fourth-horn part (in the classical orchestra the horns come in pairs, so the confusion is understandable). The player endured Scherchen's abuse, knowing that he would sooner or later recognize his error. He did but neither admitted it nor apologized: he simply changed the subject.

Anyone can make a mistake but falsely to accuse someone else of making one turns an error into a blunder. Especially as Scherchen had just impressed upon his students, who were always required to sit-in on his rehearsals, the need for a conductor to have total recall of every detail of the score. Scherchen's method of teaching was to invite his students to follow him round the world on his concert tours and simply watch him in action, following the proceedings with the aid of their pocket scores. His agent would simply hand maestro's itineraries to the students and tell them to be at a certain time in a certain concert hall in whatever country Scherchen was visiting. The ambitious young men paid Scherchen handsomely for the privilege (which every orchestral player enjoyed free-of-charge when being conducted by him). The students also, of course, had to meet all their travel and accommodation costs. But afterwards they were proudly able to add to their autobiographies, 'Studied with Hermann Scherchen'.

The students were also required to mark their pocket scores with Scherchen's comments on the proceedings. During a certain passage in Brahms's 'Tragic' Overture, Scherchen stopped the orchestra, put on a tragic face and adopted a supplicating stance like that of a Bombay beggar, arms outstretched before him, palms upwards: 'Ze oboe – *begging!*' he wailed. The oboe duly played his three notes beggingly and the conductor was satisfied. Afterwards I glanced at the score of one of the students, an American (I never knew his name though he might now be famous). He had annotated that spot, 'Oboe Begging'.

Like many conductors Scherchen had his favourite clichés which he trotted out at appropriate moments. Whenever a work he was rehearsing came to a loud, threatening passage, he would call out, 'Zis means WAR!' In spite of his rapaciousness *vis-à-vis* his students he had a great social conscience and never abandoned his left-wing views. During his Liverpool stint he spent any spare time he had left in rearranging Beethoven's Cantata for the Enthronement of Emperor Leopold II with new, Communist words (a political as well as musical blunder) and enlisted the help of some of the RLPO players for copying it out. His *Handbook of Conducting* was once a standard work but appears now to have lost some of its appeal.

2

With the greatest astonishment I beg to state that this cantata
was never composed by me. I shall retain same in my
possession in order to learn, if possible, who sent you that
kind of trash in such an impolite manner, and also to
discover the fellow who has been misusing my name.

> One Franz Schubert on receiving a copy of
> *Der Erlkönig* by *the* Franz Schubert, in 1817

Lost and found – or forged?

Every musician dreams of finding a fifth symphony by Brahms, a seventh Brandenburg Concerto which Bach mislaid, or a third set of Bach's Forty-eight Preludes and Fugues. There is often tantalizing evidence that some work was written, possibly even performed, but subsequently lost. The search for Schubert's 'Gastein' Symphony continued for much of this century, until it was proved that there had never been one: it was a case of some misinterpreted reference in one of his letters. It seems, too, that Sibelius was playing games with posterity when he hinted that an eighth symphony would be found among his effects, awaiting posthumous performance. So far none has turned up.

So much excitement – not to mention money – lies in the rediscovery of unknown works that even world-famous experts have allowed their judgement to be clouded by the euphoria of it all. But to make the front pages of newspapers – or auction rooms – a rediscovered work must be by a great composer with a documented work list, and by one who did not write too much. If another batch of unknown Vivaldi or Telemann concertos were to turn up, music lovers would yawn and remember that there were some 300-odd existing ones they had yet to hear. No one questions the genius of these composers, but their industry was so prodigious that they devalued their own stock. To discover (let alone forge) another Vivaldi concerto would be like finding (or counterfeiting) a penny piece.

Haydn forgeries became an industry even in his lifetime. He was not as easily forged as Picasso or Francis Bacon are today, but anything that bore his name sold, and publishers could not get enough of his music – so they simply hired specialists who could mimic the style. By the end of the eighteenth century more 'Haydn' than Haydn symphonies were circulating in London. Forty or more of his alleged symphonies have turned out to be by no fewer than 20 different composers, not one of them Haydn; and those figures were established before the renowned American Haydn scholar H C Robbins Landon arrived on the scene. Even the faithful old 'Haydn' Toy Symphony, in which celebrated non-musicians can make asses of themselves, is not by him but by Mozart's father, Leopold.

The busiest London counterfeiter was a disreputable Bohemian composer, Franz Kotzwara, a kind of musical 'impressionist' with a gift for mimicry, who was reputed to have assimilated Haydn's and Mozart's style 'to perfection'. In the process he helped London publishers to a fortune. Kotzwara even forged Pleyel symphonies – an irony, as some of Pleyel's genuine works were also occasionally passed off as Haydn. Kotzwara (posthumously Bohemianized by patriotic modern Czechs as Frantisek Koczwara) was hanged in London in 1791, not for forgery but for his own pleasure and by accident.

His erotic strangulation in a Soho brothel led to a celebrated scandal and well-documented murder case (but that was a different kind of blunder which you can read about in my *Wives and Loves of the Composers*).

Conversely, Haydn's D major Cello Concerto was long thought to be by his cellist friend Anton Kraft, until an autograph in Haydn's undisputed hand surfaced (though again, Haydn might have liked Kraft's concerto so much that he made a copy of it). On the other hand, another favourite Haydn work, the String Quartet from the Op 3 set, No 5, containing the delicious Serenade, has turned out to be by someone else. Alan Tyson, that great searcher after, and finder of, musical truths, says it is 'probably' by a small-time Bavarian composer called Roman Hofstetter (1742-1815). If so, why do we not hear more of someone able to write such an unforgettable tune? It should be added that on 11 January 1802 Hofstetter charmingly confessed in a letter to a friend, 'Everything that flows from Haydn's pen seems to me so beautiful, and remains so deeply imprinted in my memory, that I cannot prevent myself now and again from imitating something of his as well as I can' –

a sentiment that Samuel Butler also expressed but about Handel.

When an alleged rediscovery is brought out, one rule should be writ large on every musicologist's desk: NO ORIGINAL MANUSCRIPT, NO DEAL. Composers' hands are well known from numerous volumes of facsimiles, so one does not need to go to museums and libraries to study originals. Even when a work is claimed to be in a contemporary copyist's hand it should be possible to decide its genuineness from the way the handwriting is formed: steel nibs write differently from quills, giving an instant cut-off date. However, old, handmade and watermark-dated music paper is still occasionally obtainable (anyone fancying a bit of Beethoven forgery on paper watermarked 1797, apply here) and so are goose quills; but mixing authentic ink is more difficult, as scientists have developed smart methods of analysing its ingredients; and the use of biro is not recommended.

Musical as well as alphabetical handwriting both have clear period characteristics. The copyist of the 'Haydn' sonatas which made the headlines in 1994 and briefly fooled a few experts, wrote a neat and fluent italic hand which he could have acquired at any college of music: but as he claimed that the sonatas were not autograph but scribal he got away with it for a few days. His forgery was quickly uncovered.

People are not so easily taken in now, as they know more about musical style: more music – both printed and recorded – being available for comparison. When Kotzwara was forging Haydn 'to perfection' his work would have been adjudged perfect by his contemporaries only because they knew less of Haydn's music than we do, so it was easier to pull the wool over their ears.

From the 1920s onwards Fritz Kreisler successfully passed off what he called 'Classical Manuscripts' as works by eighteenth century masters like Couperin and Vivaldi which he claimed to have found 'in various European libraries'. He was never successfully challenged, but confessed of his own accord in 1935, saying he had delighted in making fools of experts. He was an astonishingly gifted all-round musician – in addition to being the greatest violinist of his time: how did he find the time to practise? Among his 'real' compositions, which are in a melodious but by no means simple style, are a string quartet, songs and two full-scale operettas in the Viennese tradition. He explained that as a young touring virtuoso he needed recital pieces, especially encore trifles, and did not want to keep repeating his own name on the printed programmes. That, he explained, was why he attributed the pieces to composers whose names he knew, and his audiences would know; though at that time neither he nor they were familiar with the composers' styles. Today most people, musicians as well as music lovers, know what real Dittersdorf, Pugnani, Couperin and Vivaldi sound like – and usually it is nothing like what Kreisler offered. His 'Vivaldi' violin concerto is a remarkable piece of pastiche but of a later eighteenth century style, not the Vivaldi now so familiar.

There was excitement when in 1926 a 'new' work by Schubert was published, a Quartet for Flute, Viola, Cello and Guitar. The manuscript was unquestionably in Schubert's hand and the paper on which it was written contemporaneous with him. Then someone pointed out that the work had already been printed, published and performed, though not as a Schubert Quartet but a Matiegka Trio, described as a Notturno for Flute, Viola and Guitar. Wenzeslaus Matiegka (1773-1830) was a Viennese contemporary of Schubert's who specialized in writing such pieces: there was a brisk demand for them as they were played by hired serenaders at night. Schubert had taken a fancy to Matiegka's Notturno and copied it out, at the same time adding a few bars and a part for the cello. It was probably a particular arrangement for a specific occasion (one likes to think that it might have been played under the window of a sweetheart of Schubert's – a sort of one-night *Ständchen* – and then forgotten). The players would have known they were playing Schubert's arrangement of Matiegka, so he did not bother to state a name on the music (he of all people had no need to pass off other men's music as his own). Apart from the new cello part only one passage is by him, the second Trio section of the Minuet, where he dumped Matiegka's variation and substituted his own.

If the Trades Description Act had been in force earlier, publishers would not have got away so often with murder, or rather with robbery. 'Wagner's *Nibelungen* March,' said Percy Scholes, '... impudently described on some band programmes as "by Wagner" should rather be described as "containing a little Wagner" (two short themes from *Siegfried* in the middle).' Another military-band favourite, 'Wagner's Eagle March' is genuine Wagner – not Richard but J F Wagner (1856-1908). For many Austrians he *is* the real Wagner, the famous bandmaster of the 47th and 49th regiments; his best-known works are the '*Gigerl* (or Gigolo) March' and 'Under the double eagle'. This Wagner also wrote a Flute Sonata, but it is so tuneful, simple and pleasant that it has confused no one.

Both Debussy and Ravel were involved in misattributions. The 18-year-old Claude Debussy unscrupulously passed off and published as his own the song 'Ici-bas tous les lilas meurent', although one would have thought he had even by then no need to steal someone else's work. The song was actually by Paul and Lucien Hillemacher and had already been published by them under the name of 'P L Hillemacher'. It was therefore a risky theft, but seems not to have harmed Debussy's subsequent career, though some think he should have been brought to book. Maurice Ravel's deception was in the other direction, and he merely colluded in it, for money. He composed a delightful song 'Fascination', for an outright fee to a man called Marchetti, who published it under his own name (it was featured in the film *Love in the Afternoon* and consequently gained wide popularity). Ravel was sorry later to find he had lost thousands of dollars in royalties. The song has now been restored to his authorship, and recorded on CD by Stephen Varcoe on the Hyperion label. Anyone hearing it afresh will be struck by its resemblance to 'I could have danced all night'. This was of course composed much later; but it would be wise to describe the likeness as sheer coincidence.

Misunderstandings can play their part too. Some years ago I received an anxious telephone call from my Aunt Kitty, who lived in London for nearly half a century but (like many immigrants, and especially conductors) did not feel the need to acquire a reasonable command of colloquial English. 'You are a good boy, aren't you?' she wailed, 'you wouldn't *steal* anyone else's *tune*, would you?' I was at a loss, but then she said, 'He must *hate* you, that man in the *Daily Telegraph.*' I looked at the paper and found it carried a review of an edition I had published of Mozart's Dice Game, in which he gives instructions for composing-by-chance with the help of dice. The review began with the words, 'Fritz Spiegl has stolen a march on today's aleatoric composers ...'

Will the real Franz Schubert stand up?

Franz Peter Schubert (1797-1828) was not the only musician to bear that surname. His elder brother Ferdinand Lukas Schubert (1794-1859) remained in the family's traditional calling of schoolmaster, but also composed music of his own (one or two pieces, including a Mass, are recorded). What he did not compose he filched from his late younger brother, of whose manuscripts he held custody and from which he cannibalized the odd tune for his own purposes. But then, his creativity lay chiefly in another direction: with two wives he fathered some 28 children, of whom about a dozen survived. Yet none of these Schuberts seem to have produced known descendants, except possibly unrecorded illegitimate ones.

One Franz Anton Schubert (1768-1824) was a double-bass player and composer in the service of the kings of Saxony; and his son, Franz Schubert (1808-78) followed in his father's footsteps. He was, like his father, known as the Dresden Schubert, and was principally a virtuoso violinist: only incidentally a composer. To distinguish himself from the 'real' Schubert he frenchified Franz to François. He wrote mostly drawing-room trifles for his own use, as virtuosi do. As far as published works go he can be regarded as a one-work composer (apart from some violin studies), and is known only for a little piece which the great Percy Scholes called

SOCIAL AGONIES

Anxious Musician (in a whisper, to Mrs Lyon Hunter's butler):
WHERE'S MY CELLO?
Butler (in stentorian tones, to the room): SIGNOR WERESMICELLO!

(By kind permission of *Punch*)

1895

'that busy, buzzing trifle, *L'abeille* ('The Bee'). It is a kind of 'Flight of the Bumble Bee' before its time, and a favourite encore number for recitalist fiddlers. Many editions give the name of Franz Schubert without further explanation – no doubt with the intention of passing it off as being by the 'real' one. The Schuberts never moved out of Dresden (François spent 50 years in the same orchestra) and, as Franz the Great never strayed far from Vienna, it is highly unlikely that the two families ever met.

The greatest claim to fame of the younger of the Dresden Schuberts is that he was furious when anyone asked whether he was the song composer. One – either father or son – was inadvertently sent a copy of the 'real' Franz Schubert's *Der Erlkönig* – and was furious at the thought that there might be an impostor trading on his honourable name. A letter dated 18 April 1817 goes:

> I have to inform you that some ten days ago I received a valued letter from you with which you enclosed a manuscript of Goethe's 'Erl King' alleged to have been set to music by me. With the greatest astonishment I beg to state that this cantata was never composed by me. I shall retain same in my possession in order to learn, if possible, who sent you that kind of trash in such an impolite manner, and also to discover the fellow who has been misusing my name.

The wife of the Dresden Franz Schubert, Maschinka, née Schneider (1815-82), became a celebrated coloratura soprano, and her daughter Georgine Schubert (1840-78) was also a singer, and studied with Jenny Lind and Manuel Garcia. Both were heard in London. There was also a Louis Schubert (1828-84), violinist, singing teacher and composer – no relation to any of the foregoing; but he, too, gravitated to Dresden. He composed half a dozen successful operas. To the consternation of the Nazis' race watchdogs there was also a Jewish branch of the clan, including Joseph Schubert (1757-1837), a violinist, violist and composer; and there is even a Manfred Schubert (born in Berlin in 1937) who composes 12-note serial works, though in this instance 'composed' in the past tense would probably be more accurate since the pseudo-mathematical music of the Second Viennese School is now somewhat passé. There have also been numerous musicians from the seventeenth and eighteenth centuries to modern times who bore the name Schuberth, an older spelling.

As the Great Schubert never married (some recent posthumous 'outers' have put in a claim he was homosexual), he left no known descendants, though it is likely that most sexually hyperactive men of his day – as he is said to have been, and it certainly killed him – would have produced offspring without knowing about it. It is not a *very* common name in Vienna (I don't know about Dresden) but on a visit there I saw a shop sign which read *Franz Schubert: Elektromotorenreparaturanstalt* (Establishment for the Repair of Electric Motors).

The Musical Times is hoaxed

In February 1879 the normally staid editors of *The Musical Times* were almost beside themselves with excitement, reporting that Herr Robert Franz, the distinguished German Bach expert, had visited a Schloss Witzthun in Germany and discovered a yokel,

> ... using some thin paper for tying up young trees in the garden. On looking closely he was astonished and delighted to recognize Bach's autograph. Inquiring of the gardener, he was told that the same paper filled several trunks in the attic of the mansion. Hastening thither he discovered that one trunk at least had not been rifled, and that it was full of manuscript music in the shape of 150 violin sonatas. What the other trunks contained we can unhappily only conjecture, but it is too probable that many important and long-looked-for compositions have perished at the hands of the ignorant German gardener.

Lacking the convenience of long-distance telephone or fax, *The Musical Times* editorial board had to take their informant's word for it: no chance of their hopping on a plane to see the hallowed relics for themselves. In the following issue the editors were obliged to eat their words. Not only had they been hoaxed but they had swallowed – hook, line and sinker – a story which, even with their limited nineteenth century knowledge of the works of Johann Sebastian Bach, they should have recognized as bogus. Here is where their blunder lay: the odd Bach violin sonata might have been mislaid or forgotten, and may still come to light; but that 150 of them should have sunk without trace – or ever have existed without being mentioned in contemporary accounts – was unlikely to the point of absurdity. The paper printed a somewhat ill-tempered apology.

> We regret for Herr Franz's sake, and in the interests of music, that the story was not true. We are sorry also that Herr Franz should have been so pestered with letters that, in his own words, 'the postman never left the house': and we are sorry still more that the ingenious inventor of the hoax cannot be discovered to receive the reward he deserves.

In their excitement they had failed to spot a clue in the place name: 'Schloss Witzthun' could be translated as 'Joke-making castle'.

The story resurfaced in *The Musical Times* as late as 1 September 1920, in an article entitled 'Some Musico-literary Mishaps' by Clement Antrobus Harris, who in his youth may have read (and misremembered) the news of the Bach 'discovery' but never saw its subsequent exposure as a hoax:

> Indifference is probably responsible for the loss of more manuscripts than any other cause save fanaticism. Of this Bach's works are a notable instance. On the composer's death most of his autographs were divided between his sons Friedemann and Emanuel. Those entrusted to the former

were lost, mislaid, or sold. Another miscreant was Cantor Müller (1801-90) of the Thomasschule at Leipsic. A large number of the cantatas had been left in the library of the institution, and on Müller's death all but a very small portion had vanished. In 1850, when the Bach Gesellschaft was formed, manuscripts came in from some very unexpected quarters; it is said that pages in Bach's own handwriting had been used by a gardener to tie round some young apple trees to preserve them from harm. I have read, though I cannot say where, of someone buying a pound of butter and finding that it had been wrapped up in an original copy of one of the Organ Fugues ... [and] Beethoven's cook used some sheets of the Mass in D as wrappers for superannuated pots and kettles.

Thus are hoaxes and blunders perpetuated.

The case of Pyotr Zak, Polish avant-gardist

When it comes to the music of the avant-garde, hoaxers and forgers have an easy task, as no one has any clear idea of what sounds right and what wrong. In 1961 Hans Keller, a senior producer on the BBC's Third Programme, presented a new work which he claimed to have discovered on the other side of the Iron Curtain, where dissidents were busily concocting 'degenerate capitalist western-style' art so as to annoy their commissars.

Keller and a colleague, Susan Bradshaw, had tiptoed round a deserted studio improvising on various percussion instruments that had been left in it, randomly striking a suspended cymbal here and tinkling the odd triangle there – all with the meaningful pregnant pauses obligatory in such works. Keller and Bradshaw left a recording machine switched on and labelled the resulting tape *Mobile*. Notice the snappy, one-word title, which would have been even more convincing had it been in bogus Greek followed by a meaningless Roman numeral, eg, *Mobilistikos VI* (the shelves of the Society for the Promotion of New Music are groaning under the weight of works with such nonsense titles – the compositional equivalent of the modern painter's trendily oxymoronic *Untitled*). The composer of *Mobile*, they said, was a contemporary Polish composer – a pro-western dissident, was the implication – called Pyotr Zak. Keller prefaced the recording with a typically unintelligible spoken introduction (such as can still be heard almost daily in avant-garde performances), emphasizing 'velocity graphs and decibel indexes' and no doubt offering the customary information that the music 'forms an arc' (nearly all unintelligible music seems to form an arc). This introduction lasted about three times as long as the work itself, another common characteristic of the contemporary musical scene, after which *Mobile* was duly given its first performance on Radio 3. This was followed (unusually for avant-garde works) by a second performance, though here it took place in the same broadcast, a practice sometimes followed by the BBC in premières of 'difficult' new music. No such composer exists, yet Keller fooled Radio 3 listeners as well as most critics, though some, to their credit, declared it was rubbish.

Adelaïde and the Casadesus Counterfeiting Cottage Industry

Forgeries and misattributions tend to sink without trace once they have been exposed and their true attribution established; for there is something of the wine snob in the music trade, which rejects a product when both label and date are known to be false. However, one celebrated Mozart forgery has actually entered the repertoire – the 'Adelaïde' Violin Concerto, which is in fact the joint work of the brothers Casadesus, Henri (1879-1947), Francis (1870-1954) and Marius (1879-1947), from a well-known family of French

CONVERSATIONAL INANITIES
He: OF COURSE YOU KNOW 'THE HEIR OF REDCLYFFE'?
She: I'M NOT SURE. WOULD YOU MIND HUMMING IT?

(By kind permission of *Punch*)
1887

musicians. Like the Haydn forger Kotzwara, they were gifted imitators, and moreover had the advantage of being able to work 'in committee', appraising each other's ideas: but they were not quite clever enough. Stylistically and technically alone 'Adelaïde' is a far maturer concerto than the ten-year-old Mozart could have produced, yet there are also some flat-footed, plodding passages he would even then have been incapable of writing. The brothers introduced devices Mozart could not have known but they also cunningly planted a couple of genuine fingerprints and one allusion to a genuine Mozart theme, from his *Les petits riens* ballet music. So I suspect that the Casadesus venture was based on an older source which itself contained previously forged material (it was unlikely that they would have encountered *Les petits riens* and even this suite of Mozart's includes, in its published score, some short movements he borrowed from others).

Suspicions were confirmed when Henri Casadesus refused to let anyone see the manuscript but gave the game away when he described it. He said it had been given to him by a Demoiselle Laval de Montmorency and that it was dated 'Versailles 26 May 1766', in Mozart's handwriting. In fact the Mozart family did not arrive in Versailles until two days later. Casadesus said the work was inscribed with a florid dedication to Princess Adelaïde. It was couched in a form Mozart never used; and besides, the only things Mozart formally dedicated were autograph-album inscriptions. Casadesus said the music was written in piano score – a working method Mozart never used. He wrote straight into full score, often fragmentarily dotting ideas about here and there, but invariably in its final shape – piano composition followed by subsequent scoring is a nineteenth-century practice. Another thing the forgers did not know was that Leopold Mozart proudly kept a list of his son's works: it was inconceivable that he would have omitted a violin concerto. The whole Mozart family contributed to a detailed diary in which they methodically enumerated – being inveterate snobs – every noble or influential person they saw or met, and accounted for and valued every snuffbox or watch given to them. Princess Adelaïde's dedication is not mentioned.

Nevertheless, the concerto was issued in 1933 by the reputable publishers Schott & Co, and when Paul Hindemith was asked to write a cadenza for this edition he expressed no reservations, inadvertently lending credence to a swindle. Yehudi Menuhin recorded it under the celebrated French conductor Pierre Monteux and EMI found it worthy of reissue on CD – now with a frank explanation of its provenance. Much of the foregoing evidence was discovered, known to, and revealed by, the Mozart scholar and cataloguer Alfred Einstein, who in the 1930s accused the Casadesus clan of forgery (though in the restrained language customary among scholars) and challenged them to bring out their evidence. Neither they nor their publishers replied, nor did they reach for their lawyers. But they knew they had been rumbled. They were not rogues but consummate musicians carried away by their own skills which other members of the family expressed more usefully as pianists, violinists, early-instrument makers, players of viols and violas d'amore and composers of original, non-pastiche music. This large and remarkable family founded, with Saint-Saëns, the Société des Instruments Anciens Casadesus – pioneers of what later became known as 'authentic' performances. Other 'discoveries' issued by the Casadesus production-line included a 'Handel' viola concerto, a cello concerto 'by J C Bach' and one for orchestra by 'C P E Bach' (whose styles they grievously misinterpreted). Much allegedly authentic performance is the result of half-baked theories and wishful thinking. But successful forgeries like those by the Casadesus brothers are fortunately rare.

Mr Layton hoaxes *Grove*

As the BBC's foremost expert on Scandinavian music, Robert Layton was naturally invited to be one of the chief contributors on the music of that region when the 1980 edition of the *New Grove Dictionary of Music* was being prepared – the most comprehensive musical reference work ever produced in any language, and a great achievement. But – on the principle that every good reference work should contain one hoax – Layton insinuated a 'rediscovered'

Danish musician, Dag Henrik Esrum-Hellerup, a composer who apparently led a full and productive life that spanned most of the nineteenth century (1803-91), yet had escaped the world's attention. Apparently he was a flautist, conductor and composer, son of Johann Henrik, chamber flautist to Christian IX, and had been a pupil of Johann Kuhlau; and thus far the hoax followed the sensible practice of establishing credibility by alluding to real, historical persons (just as the Casadesus forgery of 'Mozart's 'Adelaïde' concerto included a real Mozart theme).

AN ILLUSTRATION OF DARWINISM
WITHOUT USE, AN ORGAN DWINDLES; WITH USE, IT INCREASES. FOR INSTANCE, THE ORGAN OF A GRINDER WHO, IN THE STRUGGLE FOR EXISTENCE, RELIES ENTIRELY ON HIS INSTRUMENT, IS INVARIABLY LARGER THAN THAT OF THE GRINDER WHO, IN ADDITION, USES A MONKEY. MOST OF OUR READERS MUST HAVE NOTICED THIS.

(By kind permission of *Punch*)
1877

Two false clues should have given the game away. First, Hellerup's opera *Alys og Elvertøy*, ie Alice in Wonderland – no such opera is recorded in any of the opera chronologies (opera buffs are the most painstaking classifiers since Linnaeus). Secondly, people should have smelt a rat at the reference to a 'Danish translation' of the famous *Flute Treatise* by J J Quantz. The treatise was translated into several languages, and any expert on the period would have known this was a spoof. Also, those familiar with Danish railway lines would have wondered why the composer's name sounded suspiciously like a couple of stations – being the Danish equivalent of something like 'Clapham-Tooting' (and one of them produces Esrum, a famous Danish cheese).

The Danish language seems to lend itself to hoaxes, for in another *Grove* entry, this time on a real Danish composer, Pelle Gudmundsen-Holmgreen (born 1932), which was contributed by William H Reynolds, Gudmundsen-Holmgreen's 1969 composition *Preludium og Fuga* is given as 'Preludin and Fuck'. The hoax was revealed in a letter to *The Times Literary Supplement* on 1 January 1989 by one Paul Crapo (a real name of a real person, though you might not think so) from Boston, USA, who informed his readers that 'A very helpful woman at the Danish Consulate in New York City [had] assured [him] that neither the word "fuck" nor "preludin" are native to the Danish tongue.' The first of these two words most people know; and Preludin is the proprietary name of a slimming preparation, phenmetrazine hydrochloride. How it entered *Grove* is still a mystery but neither prank caused much merriment among the editors of the dictionary, who ordered reprints of the appropriate pages. Esrum-Hellerup's place is now taken by an illustration relating to a nearby entry, and the Danish title of Gudmundsen-Holmgreen's work remains untranslated. They were boyish japes intended not to mislead but to lend a little innocent merriment to a usually too-solemn subject. Yet *Grove* declared it 'a breach of trust'.

In truth such hoaxes have long been part of musical, artistic and literary life, gentle reminders to artists as well as their earnest commentators not to take themselves too seriously. Those who fell for the hoaxes need not feel ashamed: no one can be an expert in every field. Anyone who took (or takes) John Cage's 4'33" (a 'work' in three movements, all of them silent) seriously *deserves* to be called to order.

During the 1950s the celebrated television hoaxer Jonathan Routh wrote, under a pseudonym, to *The Times Literary Supplement* and various other literary journals, requesting information about 'a little-known, eighteenth-century English poet, Jeremy Feeble', on whose work he was preparing a dissertation. A little later, under different disguises, he wrote to the same papers and offered, again pseudonymously, a selection of answers. Within days he was inundated from professors of English literature all over the world (mostly at American universities); and within months Feeble had duly found a place in reference books – 'a little-known, eighteenth-century, minor English poet ... ' etc. So far none of his works has been set to music.

3

A critic is like a harem eunuch. He knows all about it but cannot do it himself.

Samuel Butler loves Handel – and no one else

Of all musical critics, one of the most narrow-minded was Samuel Butler (1835-1902), author of the novels *Erewhon, Erewhon Revisited* and *The Way of All Flesh*. Most people have certain blind spots, or develop a resistance to some composer's mannerisms or even his tricks of orchestration. But Butler suffered from what can only be described as the aural equivalent of musical tunnel vision. He was besotted by the music of Handel to the exclusion of all music written by anyone else, before or after. For Handel's works he developed a burning passion quite suddenly, when as a schoolboy at Shrewsbury he first encountered one of his compositions. He was spellbound, and no other music appealed to him for the rest of his life. He seriously believed that composers should go on writing in the style of Handel to the end of time. Henry Festing Jones, Butler's friend and biographer, wrote:

> He often tried to like the music of Bach and Beethoven, but had to give them up; they bored him too much. Nor was he more successful with other great composers; Haydn, for instance, was a sort of Horace, an agreeable, facile sort of man of the world; while Mozart – who was familiar with Handel's music and wrote pieces in homage and also composed additional accompaniments to the *Messiah* – even Mozart failed to move him.

Of a Schubert performance he wrote in his *Notebooks*: 'Then came Schubert's *Erl König* which, I daresay, is very fine but with which I have absolutely nothing in common.' Beethoven he regarded as a bombastic charlatan: 'one of the seven humbugs of Christendom'; and for Wagner he formed a positive hatred. He drew up a general list of bores, which in addition to the composers mentioned included Virgil, Goethe and the painter Raphael.

Butler put his theories to practical use by resolving to recreate the kind of music his hero wrote. He took lessons in counterpoint with W S Rockstro – with some reluctance, as Rockstro had been a pupil of Mendelssohn (though in spite of everything, Mendelssohn's influence can occasionally be discerned in Butler's compositions). But he warmed to Rockstro when he told him during the course of a lesson, 'Bach is taking niggling, restless, little irritating licences all the time for no particular reason; Handel follows the rules with loving obedience and, when he does take a licence, takes a good big one for dramatic reason, and the effect is overwhelming.' Butler wrote:

> Of all dead men Handel has had the largest place in my thoughts. In fact I should say that he and his music has been the central fact in my life since I was old enough to know of the existence of either music or life. All day long – whether I am writing or painting or walking – but always – I have had his music in my head; and if I lose sight of it and of him for an hour or two, as of course I sometimes do, this is as much as I do. I believe I am not exaggerating when I say that there has never been a day, since I was 13, without my having Handel in my mind many times over.

What Butler failed to grasp was that music had to progress with the times, or we should still be writing plainsong, just as language grew from that of Chaucer and Shakespeare. Nor was he aware that Handel himself developed through several stylistic periods within his own career, from the North German to the Italian manner; then, on first arriving in England, cultivating the Purcellian style – most notably in his glorious *Ode for the Birthday of Queen Anne* – and only then came his operatic and oratorio style, which was evidently the only kind of Handel that Butler knew. If he did have an inkling that Handelian Style was not a dead end he chose not to admit it, like someone blinded by love.

Butler wrote numerous Handelian miniatures, published in 1883 as *Gavottes, Minuets, Fugues and Other Short Pieces* for piano, but his most ambitious work was a pastoral cantata, *Narcissus,* written with the help of his friend and fellow-Handelian Henry Festing Jones, in imitation of Handel's *Acis and Galatea*. Its text gives the first – and only – indication that where music was concerned Butler actually had a sense of humour. His synopsis of the story, which is set to Handelian recitatives, arias and rousing choruses, neatly punctures his own pomposity:

> Part I: Narcissus, a simple shepherd, and Amaryllis, a prudent shepherdess, with companions, who form the Chorus, have abandoned pastoral pursuits and embarked in a course of speculation upon the Stock Exchange. This results in the loss of the hundred pounds upon which Narcissus and Amaryllis had intended to marry. Their engagement is broken off, and the condolences of the Chorus end Part I.

> Part II: In the interval between the parts the aunt and godmother of Narcissus has died at an advanced age and is discovered to have been worth one hundred thousand pounds, all of which she has bequeathed to her nephew and godson. This removes the obstacle to his union with Amaryllis; but the question arises in what securities the money is to be invested. At first he is inclined to resume his speculations and to buy Egyptian bonds, American railways, mines, etc; but yielding to the advice of Amaryllis he resolves to place the whole of it in the Three Per Cent Consolidated Bank Annuities, to marry at once, and to live comfortably upon the income. With the congratulations and approbation of the Chorus the work is brought to a conclusion.

Butler included in the cantata an instrumental interlude, or symphony, on the model of the Pastoral Symphony in Handel's *Messiah* but, unlike Handel, instructed the audience on what to do while it was played.

> Symphony: During which the Audience is requested to think as follows:

NINCOMPOOPIANA

(Surfeited with excess of 'cultchah', Prigsby and his Friends are now going in for extreme simplicity)

Prigsby: I CONSIDAH THE WORDS OF 'LITTLE BO PEEP' FRESHAH, LOVELIAH, AND MORE SUBTILE THAN ANYTHING SHELLEY EVAH WROTE. *(Recites them.)*

Muffington: QUITE SO. AND SCHUBERT NEVAH COMPOSED ANYTHING QUITE SO PRECIOUS AS THE TUNE. *(Tries to hum it.)*

Chorus: HOW SUPREME!

(By kind permission of *Punch*)

1879

An aged lady, taken ill,
Desires to reconstruct her Will;
I see her servants hurrying for
The family solicitor;
Post-haste he comes and with him brings
The usual necessary things;
With common form and driving quill
He draws the first part of the Will;
The more sustained and solemn sounds
Denote a hundred thousand pounds.

This trifle is the main bequest,
Old friends and servants take the rest.
'Tis done! I see her sign her name,
I see the attestors do the same,
Who is this happy legatee?
In the next number you will see.

Narcissus was given its first modern public performance at St John's, Smith Square, London, on 4 December 1985, the 150th anniversary of Butler's birth and also the year that marked Handel's tercentenary, in an abridged version by Robert Orledge, the present author conducting the Langham Chamber Orchestra. The abridgement was made with some trepidation, as Butler had expressed in the clearest terms (reminiscent of the words engraved on Shakespeare's tomb) his disapproval of any subsequent meddling:

May he be damned for evermore
Who tampers with *Narcissus'* score;
May he by poisonous snakes be bitten
Who writes more parts than what we've written
We tried to make the music clear
For those who sing and those who hear,
Not lost and muddled up and drowned
In overdone orchestral sound;
So kindly leave the work alone
Or do it as we want it done.

Butler himself unknowingly blundered, by lumbering his Narcissus with wildly unHandelian orchestration. All the Handel performances Butler heard in High Victorian England would have been covered in overblown nineteenth-century instrumental brown varnish, 'muddled up and drowned in overdone orchestral sound', and using anachronistic instruments like the piano and clarinets. The St John's performance 'restored' *Narcissus* – more for reasons of economy than authenticity – to what it had never been, a Handelian orchestra of strings, oboes, bassoons and harpsichord.

Bold dynamic contrasts in dull monochrome

A concert by the Orchestre de Paris, with music by Berlioz, Debussy and Beethoven, given in the Royal Festival Hall, London, under Daniel Barenboim, was noticed by *The Times* and the *Guardian*:

> *The Times* spoke of the performance's 'cumulative momentum . . .'
> The *Guardian* of 'a rough ride'.
> *The Times* of 'bold dynamic contrasts'.
> The *Guardian* thought it all 'dull monochrome'.
> *The Times* felt 'the greatest virtue of the performance was its voltage'.
> The *Guardian* that 'the orchestral execution flagged'.
> *The Times* discovered 'unprecedented strength and intensity'.
> The *Guardian* merely heard 'an exchange of coarse obscenities'.
> *The Times* had '[the orchestra playing with] swinging rhythm and bite'.
> The *Guardian* perceived 'a tired old whore flaunting too much flesh'.
> *The Times* heard 'splendidly vibrant music-making all round'.
> The *Guardian* found it 'particularly disappointing'.

The Musical Times does not like the new music for the cinema

It is fair to assume that the staid editors of *The Musical Times* earlier this century were not cinema buffs. So in 1923, before the advent of the talkies, they were astonished to find that the film industry had used music to put actresses into an appropriately tearful mood while their silent efforts were being filmed, without the sound of the mood music being heard. This was a quite separate development from the incidental music which would be added 'live' in the picture palaces during the screening by an orchestra and/or organist and which soon became a huge publishing industry only to fall away as quickly as soon as sound was added to the films at source. *The MT* wrote:

We have heard the 'Kreutzer' Sonata many a time and oft, but never once has it inclined us to tears. Yet there are evidently lachrymal properties in it, if we may judge from some newspaper paragraphs headed 'Tear Music for Film Stars'. We are told that 'the sensitive young people who act for the pictures' now scientifically exploit the possibilities of music in this way. They declare themselves unable to reach emotional peaks without the stimulus of their pet 'passion tune'. Thus Wanda Hawley, the golden-locked US star, told me that the melody she invariably employs to induce excessive sorrow is the 'Kreutzer' Sonata. Wherever she travels, Wanda's indispensable tear music accompanies her in the form of a gramophone record and a tiny portable gramophone. At the Gaumont Studios, during the week, she gave me ocular proof of her method. As she faced the camera for a pathetic scene for *The Lights o' London*, Beethoven's wailing notes murmured from the music box. Drinking in the dolorous tones the actress shivered ecstatically. A moment later pearl-like tears – indisputably genuine – welled in Wanda's eyes; the kinematographer softly turned the handle, and the touching scene was quickly completed.

So what kind of music did cinema orchestras play to evoke the mood of the silent drama unfolding? Not, as yet, specially composed music for each film. That was to come later. At first there were comprehensive libraries of background music suitable for every occasion, with indexed titles like 'Hot Pursuit', or 'Sinister Music, Russian Atmosphere' or 'Death Scene – Child' etc. The cinema orchestra conductor would have a preview of each film, then make his selection; and hand out the music to each member of the orchestra as they assembled for the showing. There was usually no rehearsal – a state of affairs that made for slapdash performances but turned the British orchestral musicians into sight-readers second to none. If specialized music was not available, the popular classics were called into service, later mechanically synchronized on celluloid. When *The Musical Times* in 1929 gently reproved Warner Bros for choosing what the editors felt was an unsuitable piece of music, they received an ironic reprimand from a reader:

> Sir, In reference to your notes ... regarding music in the cinema ... I should like you to know (because apparently you do not, nor do any of my friends who follow music with me) that Mozart's *Magic Flute* overture expresses hurry, stress, impending doom, conflicting passions, and, finally, a bridge broken by a thunderbolt, and a train falling into a ravine. You didn't know that, did you? That is because you won't be educated by Warner Bros and their huge staff, whose names take minutes to read, who have made a film called *Noah's Ark*. It is no use your saying they are wrong. This film has cost one dollar, or perhaps a million dollars, or perhaps two million dollars, and has taken at least five seconds to think out and some years to make. Therefore it must be right.

The advent of the talking pictures in the early 1930s saw the demise of the cinema orchestra and its replacement by the cinema organ, especially the Mighty Wurlitzer. It was noted for the many extra-musical effects it was able to produce, for example, thunderstorms, rain, hailstones and birdsong. Stories abound of the wrong key being pressed, resulting in a cuckoo or some such noise when the audience, in the presence of royalty, was expecting the National Anthem. *The Musical Times* hated the new-fangled instrument, and lost no opportunity of condemning it:

> 'A cinema organ properly played can be the most expressive instrument in the world, more than the human voice,' says Mr Jesse Crawford, the manipulator of the Mighty Wurlitzer at the Empire: 'When I render a number I have the words flashed on

the screen and play the notes in such a way that you can practically hear the words coming out of the organ pipes. For instance, in playing "Trees", when I come to the word "God" in the last line I pause a moment after the word and then play a distant chime. In that way I make the audience feel the words of each song.'

In August 1935 the music critic of *The MT* was sent to see *The Mystery of Edwin Drood*, newly transferred to the cinema screen. He reported:

> ... it contains much good film work, well worth seeing ... The musical joy came when the choir of Cloisterham Cathedral filed in, the service began, and after a cut we heard John Jasper, that precentor-choirmaster of rather curious provenance, begin to sing a solo; and here, with the whole acreage of sacred music to choose from, what does John Jasper pick on? A hundred guesses, and you lose every time. To my delighted ears came the first two lines, 'Where'er you walk, Cool gales shall fan the glade ...' [a popular but secular love song by Handel]; and a cool glade of chuckles fanned my neighbours. I was likely to have been sent out of *that* service in disgrace – no one among my neighbours of course batting an eyelid. After a couple of lines John staggers and falls – overcome, the producer would have us believe, by opium: but *I* know what felled him – he had suddenly realized what he was singing (somebody ought to have downed the organist, too, for he was accompanying 'Where'er'). Thus is preserved the undimmed glory of nitwittery that clothes the great cinema world, which will spend the most astonishing pains of minute care over historical detail, and solemnly commit, in any musical matter whatever, the first piece of tomfoolery that occurs to its silly mind.

A case of what *The Musical Times* called 'cinema vandalism' was brought to light in 1928 by a reader:

> In order to while away part of an afternoon I went to the

cinema. The usual kind of sentimental film was being shown, and during a scene in which, if I remember rightly, some wealthy lady was falling in love with her chauffeur, I realized suddenly that the orchestra was playing music which was vaguely familiar. Imagine my horror when I knew it to be none other than the *Et incarnatus est* from the B minor Mass! Needless to say it was being rushed through in a vulgar manner, but was nevertheless quite unmistakable.

The crude misuse of music reached its nadir with the advent of signature tunes for radio and television. Such blunders are usually brought about by producers new to classical music. One imagines them arriving in the office one morning, full of enthusiasm. 'Just heard this *fantastic* piece. Must use it.' And his next programme therefore has superimposed on it some familiar but totally unsuitable piece of music, perhaps a Beethoven sonata or the Schubert string quintet. What he does not know is that to music lovers more experienced than he the work already has its own, abstract meaning. Something of this kind must have happened when the background and signature music was chosen for *The Onedin Line*, a famous BBC television series about a nineteenth-century sailing ship. Now, whenever the first strains of Khatchaturian's 'Spartacus' suite are heard, anyone who saw the programmes is instantly transported to sea. One can hear the creaking of the ropes, the crashing of the waves, and almost feel the salt spray on their lips. Or so one believes. In reality, Khatchaturian's music is about a classical hero whose exploits formed the basis of a film about an early German Communist agitator who used 'Spartacus' as his code name.

Sir Georg Solti disappears up his own vortex

Characteristically, he whipped up the undercurrents of the slow movement into a whirling vortex, strengthening the inner string parts and driving them up to the very edge of the oboe's still, but never small, voice. When the horns and trombones announced their last movement song, it seemed a new and unexpected idea, simply because of the way Solti had prepared the ground.

The Times,
1994

Cambric handkerchiefs and a sacred oratorio

When Mendelssohn's oratorio *St Paul* was first given in Liverpool in 1836, the critic of the *Liverpool Mercury* was not too impressed by the endeavours of Madame Caradori, who had been billed as the prima donna of the evening, having been clearly imported from London in preference to a local artist, Miss Wood. He wrote:

> Madame Caradori had little to do, and that little she did carelessly. She was the nominal, and Mrs Wood the actual, prima donna of the festival. Her inattention was remarkable; one-half of the time she was forcing Mrs Knyvett to chat with her, and they diversified this by the pleasing amusement of comparing the size of their respective hands and examining the texture of their cambric handkerchiefs! This, during the performance of a sacred oratorio, was too bad!

An uneventful performance

A K Holland, the long-serving music critic of the *Liverpool Daily Post* for much of the twentieth century and a much under-rated writer, scholar and biographer of Purcell, used to say that a good critic does most of his work *before* the concert, so that he needs only to fill in the judgemental parts before telephoning his notice to his paper. He was, however, always careful not to anticipate the unexpected. If performers on the platform noticed him leaving his seat before the end of the performance (and the Liverpool Philharmonic Orchestra always gave him the same seat, a balcony gangway place, so we could all see him), he never commented on what he did not hear, not even reporting that it had been played: he always worried that there could have been a power failure, or that some thunderbolt might have struck the hall while he was safely at home and unaware of the calamity.

One of his successors left early and therefore failed to witness an event everyone else was talking about and which was reported on the news pages of the paper: namely that a deranged person had leapt from the balcony into the hall and attacked the conductor, Reginald Jacques. For the critic it had been an 'uneventful performance'. Another critic left early to retire to the Philharmonic Hotel (a splendid Victorian pub) across the road and confidently wrote: 'In Beethoven's Fifth Symphony Mr Kurtz and the orchestra had nothing new to tell us...' He was unaware that the conductor had made all repeats (unheard of in pre-authentic performances), which resulted in the playing of new 'joins' and entire passages not even the orchestra had heard before, and which left the more experienced concert goers in the audience looking at each other in amazement. During renovations in the Philharmonic Hotel in about 1950 there was discovered behind a mantelpiece a pair of complimentary tickets for a recital given in the Philharmonic Hall half a century earlier by Ferruccio Busoni (1866-1924). The tickets were unused, probably stuffed there by a critic.

A fantasy for flute

Every musician has at some time or another read criticisms of performances he never gave. If they are glowing he is in a quandary about telling the world, or quoting from them in his publicity material. I have a cutting from an American newspaper praising my playing as first flute of the Royal Philharmonic Orchestra. This would have been more gratifying had the critic not said that it was in Vaughan Williams's *Fantasia on a Theme of Thomas Tallis*. Unfortunately this work is for strings only, and Vaughan Williams was by then no longer around to be asked to add a flute part to it. The reason for such blunders is usually that the over-enthusiastic audience applauds between movements, thus leaving the less knowledgeable listener under the impression that they have applauded the end of a piece, and that the following movement is the start of the next. Thus they get hopelessly out of kilter. There are well-documented reports of concert goers wondering why the interval, which they probably longed for to socialize with their friends, was delayed by the interpolation of extra works.

But where was the critic?

Herbert Hughes (1882-1937) lost his job as chief music critic of the *Daily Telegraph* when he decided to miss a recital by the celebrated soprano Lotte Lehmann and go to a party instead. He had already made up his mind that her performance would be flawless, and filed his (already prepared) notice. Unfortunately Mme Lehmann suffered the misfortune of a sore throat and had to cancel her appearance, her place being taken at short notice by the young English singer Stiles Allen. She acquitted herself superbly well, as all the other critics agreed, while Hughes's notice in the *Daily Telegraph* wondered why 'England could offer no comparable talent to Mme Lehmann's'. And by way of a footnote: as a mere lad I was present on the platform when Miss Stiles Allen gave her last public performance, certainly her last broadcast. The performance took place in the Liverpool Philharmonic Hall and was broadcast live. The conductor was Hugo Rignold and one of her numbers was the popular coloratura aria, 'Lo, Here the Gentle Lark' by Sir Henry Bishop. This includes a florid flute obbligato, which was why I had to stand next to her at the front of the platform. In the middle of the cadenza, in which flute and voice compete, lark-like, in trills and shakes, her voice gave out, and instead of a liquid note she emitted a fearful croak, followed by an involuntary, 'Oh I'm sorry!' I nearly dropped my flute in fright and momentarily stopped, but the conductor hissed, 'Keep going!' She recovered her composure and finished the song.

Gounod's previous engagement

Gounod blundered, too, according to his biographer, James Harding:

> The dreamland in which he existed sometimes collided embarrassingly with real life. One afternoon Sir Charles Hallé gave a piano recital in Paris. That evening at a party he met Gounod, who, wrapping both his hands in a warm clasp, thanked him effusively for the pleasure the recital had given. There was one passage in particular, cried Gounod, that affected him deeply. He hummed an extract from a Beethoven sonata. 'No one, no one, my dear friend, except you, could have interpreted that passage in so masterly a way. Even with my eyes shut, I should have known that Hallé was playing.' Then Madame Gounod bustled up and apologized to Hallé for her husband's absence from the recital. He had, she helpfully explained, a previous engagement.

> From *Gounod* by James Harding (Allen & Unwin, 1973)

THE NEW CRITIC

THE 'PIZZICATO' FOR THE DOUBLE BASSES IN THE CODA SEEMS TO ME TO WANT BODY,
ALF.

(By kind permission of *Punch*)

1932

Hong Kong does not like the LPO

The *Hong Kong Standard* printed this lengthy notice of a concert in its City Hall, given in the 1970s by the London Philharmonic Orchestra conducted by Erich Leinsdorf. As is customary in tabloids, which assume that the reader has a short attention span, each sentence has a paragraph to itself, producing a curiously staccato effect:

The London Philharmonic are a noisy orchestra.

Hardworking British bulldogs, they lack grace and homogeneity.

The brass puff and blow, the flutes occasionally sound like penny whistles; even the strings are coarse.

The one outstanding section was the percussion; the timpanist was marvellous.

First came the overture to *Oberon* by von Weber.

This was a potboiler, a curtain raiser and the less said about it the better.

Then Debussy's 'Afternoon of a Faun'.

Last night's faun was an irritable beast, snapping his head from left to right, on the watch for dangers that lurked in the woods, pressed into alertness by Leinsdorf as arch-satyr.

Next came Elgar's 'Enigma Variations', spluttering a little in syncopations.

Then came the interval.

Beethoven's Fifth Symphony was an entertaining experience.

Beethoven wrote his symphony but Leinsdorf had his own ideas about its interpretation.

He wanted the slow bits slower, the fast bits faster, and the themes well and truly hammered home.

Beethoven was an ugly little man who wanted to make love not war.

Leinsdorf was determined to make a fool out of him.

Leinsdorf is a charming person, a fine technician, but most certainly not a maker of beautiful music.

With oiled shoulders he manipulated his musicians in the manner of a master-puppeteer.

He should have worn a black suit like his orchestra.

He should not have worn squeaky shoes.

The evening was an unforgettable experience.

Opinions on the Greats continue to differ

Whirlwind Jubilation in Beethoven's Ninth. *The Times*

Klemperer's Choral Tails Off: Joyless Theme. *Daily Telegraph*

A fine musical conception, and poised, elegant playing, distinguished the performance of Mozart's Thirty-ninth Symphony. *Guardian*

His account of Mozart's E flat Symphony, K543, could hardly have been duller. *The Times*

Last night in the Festival Hall, where Sir Thomas Beecham was conducting symphonies by Mozart, Haydn and Beethoven, there was a time when one feared that the whole concert was going to sleep; the Royal Philharmonic Orchestra were off their mettle. *The Times*

What is the Beecham touch? Last night at the Festival Hall Sir Thomas Beecham tried out his magic on three symphonies. Mozart's 'Haffner' and Haydn's 'Military' seemed transformed by his baton. Sparkling and fresh, these were not the performances of a veteran but of a young conductor loving music for the first time. *Daily Express*

Victorian Orchestral players – and *The Times* critic –
don't like Schubert

The conductor Sir August Manns (1825-1907), writing to *The Musical Times* in the year of his death, recalled an attempted performance of Schubert's Great C major Symphony:

> I have reason to believe that my performance of the C major Symphony in 1856 was the first in England, although I remember hearing one of the members of my then very small band speak of a rehearsal under Dr Wylde, when, at the close of the first movement, the principal horn called out to one of the first violins: 'Tom! Have you been able to discover a tune yet?' 'I have *not*,' was Tom's reply. I quote these remarks, made by two of the foremost artists in Costa's band (then the only band in England), in order to show how great was the prejudice at that time against any composition which did not come from the sanctified Haydn, Mozart, Beethoven and Mendelssohn.

What sort of a performance could it have been if a horn player, who would have opened the first movement with one of Schubert's noblest tunes for the instrument, did not recognize it as a 'tune'?

And what sort of critic was James William Davison (1813-85), founder of the *Musical Examiner* in 1842, music critic of *The Times* from 1846? He is widely considered to have been one of the foremost English critics of the Victorian era; but he, too, seems to have had a poor understanding of the man we now regard, and shall regard as long as music is sung or played, as the greatest nineteenth-century Viennese composer after (or alongside) Beethoven:

> Perhaps a more over-rated man never existed than Schubert. He has certainly written a few good songs, but what then? Has not every composer that ever composed written a few good

songs? And out of the thousand and one with which he deluged the musical world, it would, indeed, be hard if some half-dozen were not tolerable. And when that is said, all is said that can justly be said of Schubert.

Perhaps Schubert was misunderstood. Certainly by no one more than a Professor G L Scherger of Chicago, who at a Schubert Centenary Dinner held in that city in 1929 rose and said: 'It is hard indeed to account for such genius in a man who, with 19 children, received a maximum sum of $200 a year for their support.'

Strange, because Schubert never married. If he did have issue with one of his lovers, the child would not have been acknowledged – in those days the press was not as prurient as it is now. Also, since when does genius depend on a certain minimum income, and in dollars at that? Perhaps the professor, or whoever was commissioned to write his speech, confused Franz Schubert with his brother Ferdinand, who had not 19 but, it is said, 28 children, by two wives.

'Mr Smith reads the paper'

It is not often that orchestral kettledrummers gain the attention of critics, except when they are too loud. George Bernard Shaw wrote a concert notice under the above headline in the *Star* on 2 December 1889, in which he commented on the extra-musical activities of some orchestral musicians, especially when they had long rests between playing. Among these, the famous timpanist J A Smith had the habit, during concerts, of reading a big broadsheet newspaper spread out on the drums before him.

> Mr J A Smith, the eminent drum player (I would give anything to play the drum), is not the only orchestral artist who studies the press (he, I may remark, does so with such diligence that when I compose a symphony for the [Crystal] Palace, or for

Herr Richter, I shall not write in the old style, 'the drums count' but simply 'Mr Smith reads the paper'). He does not mean to annoy me, I am sure; but if he only knew how desperately I long for something to read myself during a tedious movement, he would rightly ascribe my feelings to sheer envy.

Herr Reger sits in the smallest room

This is the authentic version of a much misquoted, sometimes even misattributed, incident involving the German composer Max Reger (1873-1916). After the first performance of his Sinfonietta, Op 90, Rudolf Louis, the music critic of the *Münchener Neueste Nachrichten,* on 7 February 1906, deplored the modernity of the work, suggesting that Reger was trying to make fools of the audience. Reger was furious and wrote to Louis, 'Sir, I am sitting in the smallest room of my house. I have your notice before me. In a moment it will be behind me.' This story has been attributed to many composers – and even to Voltaire – but is authenticated by the always accurate Nicholas Slonimsky (1894-1996) in his *Lexicon of Musical Invective*; although, of course, there is always the chance that Reger copied someone else's joke.

Irving Kolodin, the critic of the New York *Sun,* wrote that 'Reger might be epitomized as a composer whose name is the same, either forward or backward, and whose music, curiously, often displays the same characteristics.'

During his short life Reger spent much time in the organ loft, renowned as the greatest German organist and contrapuntist of his time. When one of his smart pupils brought one of Reger's own organ works to him and pointed out that its dense counterpoint included a note in the middle of the keyboard which was impossible to play, as both hands and feet were fully employed elsewhere, Reger showed him how it could be done. He bent forward and played the note with his nose.

PLAY US A CHUNE, MISTER!
(By kind permission of *Punch*)
1920

Dr Charles Burney tells J S Bach and sons where they went wrong

If Sebastian Bach and his admirable son, Emmanuel, instead of being musical directors in commercial cities, had been fortunately employed to compose for the stage and the public of the great capitals, such as Naples, Paris, or London, and for performances of the first class, they would doubtless have simplified their style more to the level of their judges; the one would have sacrificed all unmeaning art and contrivance and the other been less fantastical and 'recherché', and both, by writing in a style more popular, and generally intelligible and pleasing, would have extended their fame and been indisputably the greatest musicians of the present century.

History of Music
1776

Customer: I SAY, DO YOU EVER PLAY ANYTHING BY REQUEST?
Delighted Musician: CERTAINLY, SIR.
Customer: THEN I WONDER IF YOU'D BE SO GOOD AS TO PLAY A GAME OF DOMINOES
UNTIL I'VE FINISHED MY LUNCH!

(By kind permission of *Punch*)
1929

Why Simon Rattle is a genius

By maximizing rhythmic tension at every level, Rattle created a sense of almost unbearable physical and spiritual weight. And then, liberated little by little by the second movement's dancing variations, Sibelius's tenacity was vindicated at last.

The Times, November
1994

Brahms hates Rott and Wolf hates Brahms

In 1880 the young Hugo Wolf asked Johannes Brahms for advice on his compositions, about which he felt sadly insecure. He had hoped for a little reassuring praise from the older man but Brahms, he felt, snubbed him: or at any rate Wolf, who suffered from strange changes of mood after contracting syphilis at the age of 17, interpreted the older composer's reaction as a rebuff. Although rudeness was one of Brahms's hallmarks, his abrasive manner merely hid his own uncertainties: he was a kind man at heart, without a spark of jealousy or spite in his make-up, and a devoted friend to many.

Curiously enough, Hans Rott (a supremely gifted contemporary of Wolf and Mahler) suffered exactly the same treatment at Brahms's hands – and like Wolf died insane. Rott had little time left (he died aged 25, less than four years after seeking out Brahms) and thus did not have the opportunity of taking his revenge on Brahms. Nor did he live long enough to take Mahler to task – perhaps even to court – for stealing whole chunks of his (Rott's) symphony, unacknowledged, and putting them into his (Mahler's) Symphony No 1. It would have been the plagiarism case of the century. Wolf survived until the beginning of the twentieth century and obtained a post as music critic on a Viennese newspaper, perhaps for the sole purpose of getting his own back on Brahms. It gave him the perfect vehicle for wreaking vengeance, and he never lost an opportunity of doing so. The wonder is that his editor did not stop to ask whether there might not be some ulterior motive for such sustained invective:

> In his compositions Brahms remarkably moves crabwise. He can never rise above the mediocre, yet the nothingness, the hollowness, the chickenheartedness [!] one finds in the E minor symphony has never before manifested itself so alarmingly in Brahms's efforts. The art of composition without the benefit of any musical ideas has decidedly found its most admired proponent in Herr Brahms. Just like our dear God he

understands the art of making something out of nothing. Nowadays it is taken for cleverness when a famous symphonist takes a quite modest tune and inflates it into an entire symphony. Enough of this gruesome trickery. Let Brahms be content with the thought that in his E minor symphony he has found a language which gives a mute expression to the most intensive musical impotence.

Wiener Salonblatt, 31 January 1886

Other soundbites from Wolf's hoard of poisoned invective – though we must remember that syphilis had already put him well on the way to the madhouse include such phrases as '. . . these gluey potboilings, fundamentally deceitful and twisted symphonies of Brahms ...' and, of the 'Tragic' Overture, '...the stuttering and drivelling of a musical *Macbeth*'. The *Four Serious Songs* were 'grave-digger songs'; the F major Cello Sonata 'This tohuwabohu ...'; the Violin Concerto '... a perfectly revolting piece, full of platitudes and non-thinking thoughtfulness ... a product of the torture chamber ... [of which] public performances should be forbidden by the police ...' When he was temporarily unable to think of anything bitchy enough he borrowed some of the abusive utterances against Brahms made by Wagner, who called him 'that Jewish czardas-pedlar' and claimed that Brahms, the product of a devout North German Lutheran family, was really a Jew who had changed his name from Abrahams (an absurd allegation). Hell hath no fury like a composer scorned.

O, the long and dreary poem!

In 1927 the *Daily Telegraph* sent its music critic to cover a performance of *Hiawatha's Wedding Feast* by Samuel Coleridge-Taylor in the Free Trade Hall in Manchester. The Hallé Orchestra was conducted by Sir Henry Wood, with a team of distinguished soloists that included Stiles Allen, the tenor Arthur Jordan, and the baritone Roy Henderson, who after he retired from the concert platform went on to become one of the most sought-after singing-teachers: his pupils read like one great roll of fame, including Kathleen Ferrier, John Shirley-Quirk and almost anyone else who made a name in opera or song. *Hiawatha* was once immensely popular in England and Wales, and regularly featured in British concert halls, both in London and the north, with an annual staged performance in costume in the Royal Albert Hall, conducted by the composer's daughter Avril Coleridge-Taylor. The *Telegraph* critic loved the Manchester performance but hated the work, breaking into verse in imitation of Longfellow's poem. This is a slightly shortened, edited version:

Hiawatha in fitting fashion

Brilliant Rendering of Dreary Work
'Very Earnest'

You shall hear how *Hiawatha*
Set to music (Coleridge-Taylor's)
Was performed in fitting fashion
At the final Brand Lane Concert
In the mighty Free Trade Wigwam,
Vast and gloomy Free Trade Wigwam,
How Roy Henderson the mighty,
He, the sweetest of musicians,
Sang his songs of love and longing;
How the tenor, Arthur Jordan,
Sang with force, but not so sweetly;
And Miss Lilian Stiles Allen
Sang in accents soft and tender
Sang (with rather much vibrato)
Songs of love and lamentation.

First the audience assembled,
Muffled in their thickest raiment:
In their thickest raiment muffled,
Fit for Manchester in winter
(And for Manchester in summer)
Splendid in their paint and plumage.
Then Sir Henry Wood, conductor,
He, the black-robed chief, the paleface
(And with hair his chin was covered),
Rose to stimulate the chorus:
'Give me of your bark, O basses
Of your mellow bark, O tenors!
Lift your voices, O sopranos!
O sopranos, lift your voices.
Life is real. Life is earnest.
Life is really very earnest.'
And the choir, the Philharmonic,
And the orchestra, the Hallé,
Toiling – sorrowing – rejoicing,
Leaped to meet him, leaped to meet him
As the Laughing (Soda) Water
Springs to meet the amber whisky
In the clubs when nights are brightest,
Sweetly sang the muted oboe,
Calling to his mate, the cello,
From the branches of the woodwind.
And the *Song of Hiawatha*
Reached a high, exalted level.

O, the long and dreary poem!
O, the tedious cantata!
Art is long and life is fleeting:
Very long is *Hiawatha*;
Far too long is *Hiawatha*.
And before the work was over

We had lost the way of smiling,
And our hearts were sad and darkened,
As the River Irwell darkens
When the boys drop bottles in it.
Long before the work was over
(And despite a fine performance)
We were ready to consign it
To the Islands of the Blessed,
To the Kingdom of Ponemah,
To the Land of the hereafter.

Lift your voices, O sopranos!
O sopranos, lift your voices.
Life is real. Life is earnest.
Life is really very earnest.
And impatient is the audience.
'On! Away! Awake, beloved!'

Brahms and Tesco

Brahms's Second is not about verdant hills or bucolic swains; it is about the Great Chain of Being, the disappearance of the Great Auk, Harold Macmillan's cat Maxwell, the Harmony of the Spheres, the Alliance and Leicester 12-year index-linked equities package, sex, the curse of Tutankhamoun, the Whirligig of Life, the fourth urinal from the left in the gents' loo at Kings Cross Station, 'The Hunting of the Snark', the Tesco Five Items or Less (no credit cards) counter, *The Taming of the Shrew*, the rise of the *vihuelistas* in fifteenth-century Spain, the fall of the Ottoman Empire, the electrification of the Soviet Union, the emancipation of the bourgeoisie, total groove.

So declared the writer of a programme note for a concert at King's College, Cambridge, in 1993. Brahms's Second Symphony is possibly also about the consumption of certain substances, such as alcohol, etc, which cloud the mind and give a student the impression that banal ideas are imbued with flashes of infinite insight.

Johann Sebastian Bach fails to catch on

Bach's *Passione* is much more talked about than known; and our acquaintance with the score leads us to be wary of the enthusiasm of its wholesale admirers, who place it far above the works of Handel.

Musical World, May 1845

A selection from the *Passions-Musik* of Johann Sebastian Bach, from the manner in which it was announced in the programme, was evidently designed to be one of the most prominent points of the concert. But it failed to produce the expected effect; it was found dry and heavy, and very coldly received. Bach is a great and time-honoured name; but his vocal music is very little known in England, and what is known hardly seems to justify the veneration of his classical admirers.

Illustrated London News, April 1854

From an artistic point of view I put little value upon the logical demonstrations in sound worked out by John Sebastian Bach. I do not consider them, from a musical point of view, to be any superior to the mathematical demonstrations made by a good professor at any European university.

W J Turner, *The Musical Times*, December 1932

It will, of course, be a long time before the intricate music of Bach can be properly and effectively executed; and when a

MC of village concert (to famous pianist): PERHAPS I OUGHT TO TELL YOU, SIR, THE WIRELESS 'AS MADE US ALL PRETTY CRITICAL 'ERE IN LITTLE WORTLEBURY.

(By kind permission of *Punch*)

1933

thoroughly efficient ensemble is secured, it will still be doubtful whether the *Passione* according to St Matthew or St John can ever be permanently retained in the oratorio repertoire.

The Atheneum, 18 February 1871

Bach dismays players

In 1838, Lord Burghersh, later Earl of Westmorland ('that very musical peer', *The Musical Times* called him) who was a composer, the founder of the Royal Academy of Music, and director of Ancient Concerts (London's first organization devoted to the revival of early music), mounted an experimental performance of the music of Johann Sebastian Bach. Again, Bach failed to impress the *Musical World*:

> The chorus is accompanied, we believe, by three obbligati trumpets, the alto tromba extending to E [actually D] in alt. This part of course Mr Harper could not play, nor indeed could anybody, with the instrument now in use in our orchestras. The aria '*Qui sedes*', has an obbligato accompaniment for the tenoroon [!] or oboe d'amore, an instrument which extended below the Corno Inglese [actually above it]. This Mr Grattan Cooke attempted on the common oboe, and of course stopped at the very outset of his exertions. The bass solo, '*Quoniam tu solus*'. is accompanied by a corno and two fagotti. The passages for the horn were next to impracticable, and Mr Denman was furnished with a fagotti part which appeared greatly incorrect. Of course the selection was slaughtered, the soli players retiring in dismay, leaving Mr Knyvett to play their parts on the organ, which he did most manfully ...

George Bernard Shaw pans the 'infinitesimal Grieg'

For some years the playwright George Bernard Shaw acted as music critic of the London newspaper the *Star*, contributing anonymously some of the most amusing, perceptive and enlightening (sometimes invective-laden) reports ever written about metropolitan concert life. He was opinionated to a degree and suffered from a few blind spots that seem strange to us – about Tchaikovsky and Brahms, for example. Mozart was his god, to whom he prayed every day.

In general GBS approved of Edvard Grieg, but when he discovered that the Norwegian had committed the unpardonable sin of arranging some of Mozart's music, his fury knew no bounds. And what had Grieg done? He had merely amused himself by adding counterpoints – additional tunes – to some of Mozart's piano works, as Schumann and Moscheles had done to Bach, and Gounod also did when superimposing his famous 'Ave Maria' on the already self-contained first Prelude of Book I of the 'Forty-eight'.

In truth such an exercise often shows great contrapuntal ingenuity and does no harm to the original: it is no worse than painting a moustache on a print – not the original painting – of Leonardo da Vinci's *Mona Lisa*. Grieg's attempts at 'improving' Mozart – whose music no one could accuse of being un-self-contained – are indeed absurd to the point of ridiculousness, because they manage to clothe eighteenth-century piano classics in nineteenth-century Norwegian folk costume. Indeed several passages in them are guaranteed to move any knowledgeable audience to spontaneous bursts of laughter – something few musical works can do; and Grieg took it all seriously enough to 'improve' the great C minor Fantasia as well as several sonatas.

GBS did not see it as an ingenious musical *ésprit* but a permanent desecration of a shrine. On 7 March 1890, he reported on a recital by a famous Norwegian pianist, Agathe Backer-Grøndhal which, he said, threw him into ...

...a perfect frenzy of exasperation. Do you know that noble Fantasia in C minor, in which Mozart shewed what Beethoven was to do with the pianoforte sonata, just as in *Das Veilchen* he shewed what Schubert was to do with the song? Imagine my feelings when Madame Backer-Grøndahl, instead of playing this Fantasia (which she would have done beautifully), set Madame Haas to play it, and then sat down beside her and struck up 'an original part for the second piano', in which every interpolation was an impertinence and every addition a blemish. Shocked and pained as everyone who knew and loved the Fantasia must have been, there was a certain grim ironic interest in the fact that the man who had the unspeakable presumption to offer us his improvements on Mozart is the infinitesimal Grieg. The world reproaches Mozart for his inspired variation on Handel's 'The People that Walked in Darkness'. I do not know what the world will now say to Grieg; but if ever he plays that 'original second part' himself to an audience equipped with adequate musical culture, I sincerely advise him to ascertain beforehand that no brickbats or other loose and suitably heavy articles have been left carelessly about the room.

And cannot get hold of Johannes Brahms

The other day a small but select audience assembled in one of Messrs Broadwood's rooms to hear Miss Florence May play a pianoforte concerto by Brahms. An orchestra being out of the question, Mr Otto Goldschmidt and Mr Kemp played an arrangement of the band parts on two pianofortes. Brahms's music is at bottom only a prodigiously elaborated compound of incoherent reminiscences, and it is quite possible for a young lady with one of those wonderful 'techniques', which are freely manufactured at Leipzig and other places, to struggle with his music for an hour at a stretch without giving such insight to her higher powers as half a dozen bars of a sonata by Mozart. All that can be said confidently of Miss May is that her technique is undeniable. The ensemble of the three Broadwood grands was not so dreadful as might have been expected, and the pretty 'finale' pleased everybody.

Star,
18 December 1888

It may come as a surprise to those who read the splendid two-volume *Life of Johannes Brahms* by Florence May (1845-1923) that the author of the most authoritative important English biography of the composer was a pianist in her own right. In fact she was a kind of English Clara Schumann. Her father, like that of Clara (née Wieck), was a celebrated piano teacher but, being less draconian than Friedrich Wieck, sent her for lessons to Mme Schumann. Through her she met Brahms and became a fervent disciple and friend – some said also his lover. For many years she was considered the perfect interpreter of Brahms's music. Her accompanist on the occasion George Bernard Shaw wrote about was Otto Goldschmidt, a noted conductor and composer of his day (and husband of Jenny Lind); so Shaw was attacking no mere nonentities. Half a century later he acknowledged the foolishness of that criticism – though even then he failed to understand that Brahms's musical language was, and remains, the most uneclectic, the most immediately and idiomatically recognizable, of all composers of his time:

> The above hasty (not to say silly) description of Brahms's music will, I hope, be a warning to critics who know too much. In every composer's works there are passages that are part of the common stock of the music of the time; and when a new genius arises, and his idiom is still unfamiliar and therefore even disagreeable, it is easy for a critic who knows that stock to recognize its contribution to the new work and fail to take in the original complexion put upon it. Beethoven denounced

Weber's *Euryanthe* overture as a string of diminished sevenths. I had not yet got hold of the idiosyncratic Brahms.

Worse than influenza

A performance by the Bach choir also left GBS feeling unwell:

> To Prince's Hall to hear a concert given by the Bach Choir at the eccentric hour of half past five. Unaccompanied part-singing was the staple of the entertainment; and I can frankly and unreservedly say that I would not desire to hear a more abominable noise than was offered to us under pretext of Bach's *Singet dem Herrn* and some motets by Brahms. I will not deny that there was a sort of broken thread of vocal tone running through the sound fabric; but for the most part it was a horrible tissue of puffing and blowing and wheezing and groaning and buzzing and hissing and gargling and shrieking and spluttering and grunting and generally making every sort of noise that is incidental to bad singing, severe exertion and mortal fear of losing one's place. It was really worse than the influenza.

The World,
20 May 1891

His powerful performance was oddly lifeless and lacking in character

The clarinettist produced an anxious, insubstantial tone that was in danger of vanishing altogether. *The Times*

The clarinet player drew from his instrument nearly all the loveliness enshrined there by Mozart. *Guardian*

MUSIC OF THE FUTURE

MUSIC BEING TAUGHT NO LONGER BY THE EAR, BUT BY THE EYE EXCLUSIVELY (AND FORMING A PART OF COMPULSORY EDUCATION), ORGAN GRINDERS ARE SUPERSEDED BY PERIPATETIC PROFESSORS BEARING THE PRINTED SCORES OF THE BEST MASTERS, AND BEATING TIME AS THEY TURN THE LEAVES.

Shoe-black (reading): YES, BUT I THINK HE'S TAKING THE TEMPO TOO 'ACCELERATO'!

Shoe-black (reading): HEAVENLY ADAGIO, AIN'T IT, BILL?
Crossing sweeper: YES, BUT I THINK HE'S TAKING THE TEMPO TOO 'ACCELERATO'!

(By kind permission of *Punch*)

1878

Everything [in Giulini's conducting] was kept tense and vital, yet every detail was given time to expand to its full lyrical and dramatic stature. It was a powerful performance which engulfed the listener more and more with its growing momentum.   *The Times*

[Giulini's] performance was oddly lifeless, and lacking in character. There is no tension in it, no sense of dramatic situation.   *Financial Times*

Of a performance of Bach's Double Concerto in D minor, given at the Royal Festival Hall by the Russian violinists David and Igor Oistrakh, father and son:

Two well-differentiated tones, the father's sweeter and more silvery, the son's weightier and more penetrating.   *Guardian*

Mr Oistrakh, senior, had the more penetrating, his son the more silvery, tone.   *The Times*

Mr Tolhurst writes an oratorio down under

In May 1864, London received news of a new oratorio composed in a far-flung corner of the British Empire, news which was as unexpected as it was encouraging. The editors of *The Musical Times* were delighted – if a little patronizing:

The production of a new oratorio at the antipodes is an event which must interest all who watch with pleasure the spread of music as a humanizing influence throughout the civilized world. We learn from the *Melbourne Argus* that at the Town hall, Prahran, a suburb of Melbourne, Australia, an oratorio called *Ruth* has been lately produced, the composition of Mr George Tolhurst, a professor of music resident in the neighbourhood, and, we are happy to add, with complete success. As this is the first oratorio that has been composed in the colony, it will no doubt act as an incentive to other resident musicians; and materially aid in promoting an artistic competition which may eventually lead to good results.

Most people in the mother-country were convinced that Australia was still inhabited largely by convicts and sheep-shearers, who could well do with a bit of civilizing. Communications were slow, so it took another four years before a copy of the oratorio (loyally dedicated to Queen Victoria) reached *The Musical Times* for critical consideration. A review by an Australian music critic had already described the work as being '... of the highest excellence [and] betokens no ordinary genius in the composer ...' This had whetted *The MT* editors' appetites.

Tolhurst was certainly no ordinary genius, and the backwash from *Ruth* was to make waves in *The Musical Times* until 1920. Indeed the work is still occasionally performed, which is more than can be said for most of the compositions of all those Victorian composers to whom knighthoods were handed out like confetti.

The first London performance of *Ruth* took place in March of the same year, in the Store Street Concert Room, with some of the most famous names on the metropolitan concert scene taking part with great gusto. In the following year another performance was organized in Maidstone, Kent, and *The Musical Times* quoted the music critic of the *Maidstone Telegraph* as saying that 'every piece was vociferously cheered'.

Another performance was noticed in *The Monthly Musical Record* of June 1872 by none less than the great teacher of harmony, counterpoint and musical form, Ebenezer Prout. Prout singled out a '... most remarkable movement, which contains some striking passages, quite unlike anything to be met with in the whole range of music ... a chorus of no common order ... to which no verbal description can possibly do justice.' He wrote a perfectly serious, extravagantly laudatory, criticism which the composer took perfectly seriously – and wrote from Australia to thank him.

But in fact all the English performances had been given in fun, so that the performers – and no doubt the audiences – could have a good laugh at Tolhurst. In other words, it was a *succès de ridicule* which London had exploited to the full. Tolhurst, poor man, had only been doing his best: the only trouble was that his best was not very good. Curiously enough the editors of *The MT* had written about the work in a more serious vein, before they had seen its comic possibilities, in February 1868: 'We know nothing of Mr Tolhurst and should have been pleased to know nothing of his oratorio . . . the choruses appear to be the work of a student groping his way in part-writing and . . . are in some portions perfectly unendurable.'

I was able to get hold of a score of *Ruth* and organized performances of excerpts – although, like all repetitively incompetent music, its effect soon palls. But was the Australian joke perhaps meant at the expense of the rest of the world? Mr Tolhurst was clearly in the most avant forefront of the foremost avant-garde, a minimalist before his time. Those of today's critics who approve of the minimal talents of minimalists like John Adams, Steve Reich and Michael Nyman would probably have praised Tolhurst to the skies. Film producers, had there been any, would have fallen over each other to commission works from him, and for a time the mere appearance of the name Tolhurst ('George Tolhurst and the Tolhurst Band play Tolhurst') would have packed concert halls. And no one would have laughed, except Tolhurst on his way to the bank. Like some of our mini-talented composers he knew how to spin out the tiniest ideas for a very, very long time. As *The Musical Times* wrote in January 1920, in terms that might have been equally apt 70 years later for twentieth-century minimalists:

> Tolhurst sets out to give us a picture of daybreak. A somewhat lengthy extract is necessary to show how he gradually piles up his effect until we emerge from the chill of dawn into the full blaze of day. The material is simple enough, yet how cumulative is the result! No audience can fail to be moved by such writing as this.

Again the editors of *The Musical Times* had their tongue firmly in their cheeks, and concluded:

> We have here a work which is a credit to native art. Beyond doubt the musical future of our race rests chiefly in the hands of composers of such works as this. We welcome Mr Tolhurst as a newcomer into a field he is certain to adorn. That *Ruth* will not be his last work is certain, for we hear that he has almost finished an oratorio on the story of Balaam. We are assured by a mutual friend that this marks an advance on *Ruth*. The composer's great natural gift for descriptive writing has full play in the passage relating to Balaam's journey. Our friend tells us that he has rarely been so affected by any music as by the aria of the Prophet's faithful and ill-used beast, a setting (given with sure instinct to the tenor) of the words 'Am I not thine ass?'

Don't listen to Debussy

Better not listen to him: one runs the risk of getting accustomed to him, and one might end up by liking him.

> Rimsky-Korsakov, on Debussy

There is no hope for *Cosi fan tutte* on the stage as the work stands.

> H F Chorley, music critic, 1808-72

He is verye often drunke and by no means thereof he hath by unorderlie playing on the organs putt the quire out of time and disordered them.

> The Dean and Chapter of Lincoln Cathedral,
> on Thomas Kingston, organist,
> 1599-1616.

Critics – take heed

Pour not out words where there is a musician, and show not
forth wisdom out of time.

Apocrypha

4

These instruments invite playing in Winter ... they encourage practice ... by a gentle warmth rising from two small hot-water cylinders ... comfort and perfect suppleness of hands are thus ensured; practice becomes inviting; pupils willing ... and the Piano an article of unmixed pleasure ...

Mr Price's Patent Piano Warmer, 1869

The piano poses as furniture

One of the dottier names invented by the piano industry is the Boudoir Grand, a relative of the Baby Grand. I have known many pianos kept for lack of other space in the bedsitting-rooms of students or young professionals; but never met a lady so grand that she sleeps in a 'boudoir', yet has nowhere else to keep her piano. There was, however, a 'dormitory piano' patented in 1866 by a Mr Milward. In addition to the usual arrangements it housed a fold-down bed with a mattress, washbasin, jug and looking glass; as well as a closet for the bedclothes.

In 1893 *The Musical Times* quoted part of a piano seller's advertisement which takes us back, if not to the boudoir or the bedroom, at least to a secluded corner of a drawing-room designed for what the paper called 'whispering lovers'. Here is the advertisement in full, complete with every gushing adjective, getting increasingly manic as its author warms to the subject; and is quite unable to stop.

> Placed near a bay window [the pianoforte] shuts in the cosiest lovers' nest imaginable. Soft-cushioned window seats that have room for just two – intuitive seats they might be called – are hidden thus away completely from the cold, cruel world. Little couches may be hidden in the shadow of such a piano when rich hangings fall from a corner window. Or a delightful tea corner is made with a screen for a doorway, and soft divans and dim lights inside. Or the back of the piano [we are here clearly talking of an upright model] may be hung with a soft shade of yellow, brocaded with dull green leaves and flowers. Against this a little tea-table can be placed, with its dainty belongings, and a low chair beside it. A yellow-cushioned divan can extend entirely around this corner, lighted by the soft radiance of a lamp with a pale green shade, and piled high with a baker's dozen of pillows – large and small and medium – with bright silken covers.

TO SOLVE THE SERVANT PROBLEM
THE COMBINATION PIANOLA-STOVE
(By kind permission of *Punch*)

Patent Office Specifications reveal a constant quest for improvements in keyboard instruments, from practical devices 'to prevent the ingress of mice into the mechanism' (also useful for organs and harmoniums) to centrally heated pianos. Such instruments were fitted with Mr Price's Patent Piano Warmer of 1869, and are reminders of how cold English Victorian houses must have been during the winter. No wonder children dreaded their daily piano practice:

> These Instruments invite playing in Winter when the coldness of the keys of all others makes it unnecessarily uncomfortable, if not painful, to many, especially children. They encourage practice, and facilitate execution, by a gentle

warmth, rising from two small hot-water cylinders, of only the diameter of a wine-glass, hidden under their ends, easily handled, and giving a temperature *never above* blood-heat, and *averaging* summer heat for three hours. Comfort and perfect suppleness of hands are thus ensured; practice becomes inviting; pupils willing; the master's time economized; progress uninterrupted; general playing agreeable; and the Piano an article of unmixed pleasure; and most useful, when, in winter, from the absence of outdoor amusements, it is most wanted, but is now most avoided ...

There were also conductors' pianos (really glorified music desks with a four-octave keyboard and intended presumably for conductors unable to communicate their wishes by singing); pianos with organ attachments; cottage pianos; church pianos (encased in carved oak and bound in gleaming brass, to harmonize with the ecclesiastical furniture); yacht pianos (presumably small and water-resistant); and pianinos – first named in 1862 in a non-proprietary way but later officially adopted for a small Steinway. The most far-reaching in its influence – though in a strictly non-musical way – was Mr W G Eavestaff's Minipiano, a trade mark registered in 1934. His instrument was based on a Swedish prototype made in 1932 by the firm of C A V Lundholm and was less than a metre high, beating the Steinway Pianino by 30 centimetres. The Minipiano became almost a fashion accessory, 'made to harmonize with every type of decoration'; could be obtained 'streamlined and cellulosed to suit the ultra-modern flat ...' The care that went into its 'contemporary' styling was doubtless later lavished on radiograms, and later still on television sets. It is not generally acknowledged that we owe to Mr Eavestaff, not Morris, Austin and the British Motor Corporation, the useful mini prefix, from mini cars to mini cabs (1961) and mini skirts (1966), to minikinis and mini-everything-else. Curiously enough, there was also an Italian composer called Alessandro Mini (c 1756-1825) – a small talent maybe, but he did get into *Grove's Dictionary of Music*.

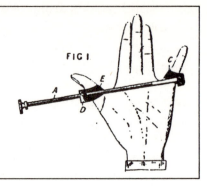

7115. Crane, F. L. April 4.

Exercising-apparatus, particularly for use by piano players. Loops E, C are placed over the portions of the hand required to be stretched, and are thrust apart by the screwed rod A, which passes through a nut D carried by one of the loops.

FIG I

Strauss and Mengelberg endorse the windbag

Professional musicians are conservative by nature. Having perfected their technique and maintained it by constant practice, they are unwilling to learn new tricks. It is usually the ingenious amateur who proposes a fundamental revision of music notation, a change of layout in the piano keyboard, or adds new keys and gadgets that claim to take the sweat and toil out of wind-playing. The professional rejects them because he cannot afford to suspend work while fundamentally re-learning and re-training.

An inventor who did succeed in getting his revisions accepted was Theobald Boehm (1794-1881), a goldsmith and ironmaster as well as flautist, whose revolutionary alterations to the mechanism of the flute did eventually prevail, and he rewarded their efforts of re-learning by giving them an instrument that was easier to play.

Another metalworker-flautist with a revolutionary idea for taking some of the effort out of wind-playing was less successful. Although he persuaded the greatest conductors of his day to furnish him with testimonials, his colleagues refused to make idiots of themselves on the platform by attaching themselves to his unwieldy apparatus. He was Bernhard Samuels, born on 10 November 1872 in Paramaribo, Dutch Surinam. His early training was as a goldsmith and diamond worker, but his father taught him the flute and he eventually joined the Amsterdam Concertgebouw Orchestra. In 1904, he moved to Essen, where his playing came to the notice of the composer Max Reger and the conductor Felix Mottl, whose recommendations secured him a position as first flute for the Bayreuth Festival. In 1912 he patented his Aerophor (not 'Aerophone', as sometimes misspelt) a device designed to ease the lot of wind-players having to blow long phrases without an opportunity for taking breath. It consisted of a pair of bellows worked with the foot and supplying air to the corner of the player's mouth through a long rubber tube.

Like most inventions (even Boehm's famous 'system') it was a modification of previous ideas: the Aerophor originated in an industrial apparatus patented in France in 1877 called the Aerophore, 'which enables the miner to carry sufficient air for his own respiration', a sort of simple breathing apparatus. Samuels's Aerophor supplied air only to the mouth of the player, not to his lungs; and without the supporting action of the player's diaphragm, so important in blowing wind and brass instruments, it could have been of little use. Even less clear is how the other members of an orchestra managed to play while laughing their heads off at colleagues tubed up like accident victims while at the same time pedalling away at a pair of bellows and trying to play the music in front of them. Like many absurd musical inventions the Aerophor would have been forgotten had not Richard Strauss stipulated its use in his Alpine Symphony, Op 64 (1911-15) and his *Festliches Praeludium*, Op 61 (1913), an inclusion now always ignored:

> My heartiest thanks to Herr Bernhard Samuels for his epoch-making invention. I hope that this will shortly be introduced into all orchestras. With it begins a new era in orchestral technique.
>
> Dr Richard Strauss, Garmisch, 15 April 1912

> Very honoured Herr Samuels!
> Your apparatus for continuous sound is a magnificent invention, not to say one of genius. Equipped with your

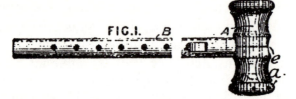

28,149. Starck, E. E. Dec. 9.

FIG.1. B A

Flageolets ; whistles ; music notation. — The instrument is in the form of, and may be used as, a chairman's hammer for convivial gatherings. The handle B constitutes a flageolet or whistle, and may be detached from the head A and used separately, or it may be blown into through an opening e in the head which is hollow. The end a of the head is detachable, and has holes k leading into

apparatus, an orchestra becomes a living organ. I look forward even now to the pleasure of conducting such a long-breathed orchestra, and hope that soon all orchestral wind-players will make music with your apparatus.

To the listener, the taking of breath is totally imperceptible: the air-stream continues, endlessly and without limitation, whether in long notes, long melodic phrases, moving passages, etc.

For example, I heard an oboist play for half an hour without interruption, and afterwards the gentleman was as completely fresh (no rush of blood to the head, no increase in pulse rate) as if he had not so much as breathed into his instrument.

W Mengelberg, Amsterdam, 6 September 1911

I wonder whether Samuels was aware also of an even earlier effort, by:

... the late Mr Samuel Hogben the surgeon who, being in delicate form, and subject to cough, found that playing the flute affected his breathing ... so that he found it necessary, in order to continue the gratification which he derived from this instrument, to contrive an *artificial breath* for it. This he accomplish't *so perfectly and conveniently*, that he could *sing and play at the same time* ...

Gentlemen's Magazine, September 1815

Unfortunately Dr Hogben's Patent Wind Machine met the same fate as Mr Samuels's Aerophor. A still more unlikely invention than the Aerophor was offered by a M Isonard of Paris in 1926, though he was apparently unable to persuade the famous conductors of his day to testify to its effectiveness:

A Violin played by a Pair of bellows: The performer holds the instrument after the manner of a violoncello: his feet work the bellows (like a knife-grinder) and his right hand directs the stream of air to the string requiring it.

The Musical Times

Inventors name names

The boom in instrumental inventions during the nineteenth century and the consequent need for new names produced some interesting etymological curiosities, and not a few blunders. Many are named after their inventors, or include part of his name in some ingenious manner; others are named after the composers who promoted them, like the Wagner Tuba; others again after bandmasters who used them, like Sousa, who lent his name to the Sousaphone, which is not only played but worn, keeping the player warm with what looks like a series of coiled central-heating pipes.

The old German firm of Wilhelm Heckel, long famous for its bassoons, also made other instruments. These include the Heckelclarind – the only instrument named after a typographical error: it should have been the Heckelclarina, but its misprinted final letter caught people's imagination and it stuck. In 1879, Herr Heckel was summoned into Wagner's presence and ordered to make him a baritone oboe for use in *Tristan and Isolde*, which he did; and, doubtless to the Master's chagrin, he called it not the Wagner Oboe but the Heckelphone. Richard Strauss, always a believer in instrumental novelties, having endorsed the Aerophor, used a Heckelphone in *Salome*. There are not many about in the profession, and they tend to be hired for special occasions rather than owned, so they have not exactly set the musical world on fire. The name has always sat uneasily on English lips, suggesting some kind of megaphone for use at elections (presumably the Heckelphone has now been joined by the Heckelfax). Indeed there was an American invention called the Tuba Stentorophonica, which was a kind of musical speaking tube and might be worth reviving for election meetings.

Wagner did, however, have a set of tubas (actually saxhorns) named after him. In 1853, he visited the workshops of Adolphe Sax and discussed with him the possibility of having some special instruments made for use in his operas, a cross between horns and tubas. Sax obliged, and Wagner was delighted. They are used to splendid effect in *Das Rheingold* and *Götterdämmerung*, producing a rich and smooth sound, and are usually played by horn players (who in the gloom of the opera pit look for all the world as if they had four brassy women sitting in their laps). Bruckner, in his later symphonies, Stravinsky and Strauss, also called for them, but their scarcity and hiring expense has prevented their spread into the standard repertoire. Wagner, however, missed a trick by not summoning the instrument-maker Cerveny who, in 1846, patented the *Schwanenhorn*, or swan's horn, which might have looked good in *Lohengrin*.

It is usually the brass instruments that have the most extravagant, imaginative or evocative, names, most but not all named after their inventor. We know well the saxophone, the saxhorn and other instruments named by Adolphe Sax: everyday words, yet journalists and publicity people find them a source of naive wonder, with endless headline puns on 'sex': the Fairer Sax, Sax Appeal, etc. The Ophicleide was a giant-keyed bugle, sometimes given a monster serpent's head at the bell end. Its name comes from the Greek words for serpent and key, respectively, and its tone was compared (by the *Musical World* in 1841) to a 'hog-song'; while Berlioz likened it to a 'chromatic bullock' (or was it Monsieur Sarrus's Sarrusophone he was thinking of?).

The tuba confusion goes back all the way to biblical times, or at any rate biblical translation. The Latin *tuba* refers to the straight bronze war trumpet of the ancient Romans; therefore *Tuba mirum spargens sonum* in the Latin Mass refers to the putative sound of the last trumpet, at the first fanfare of which, it is claimed, we shall all be raised. However, in many famous musical settings of the passage the obbligato instrument used at that point is either the trumpet or a trombone, because the orchestral tuba was not invented until the middle of the last century. Mozart further confused the issue by giving Handel's famous trumpet part in *The Messiah* to the horn; and in standard performances of Handel's oratorio, where the baritone's recitative heralds the event with the words, 'At the *last* trumpet' it is the *first* trumpet who stands up to deliver his obbligato.

Clifford Bevan's book *The Tuba Family* lists hundreds of brass-instrumental inventions, a veritable minefield for the etymologist and the patent office clerk alike, but indicative of the industry and imagination that went into instrumental innovations, most of which unfortunately turned out to be well-meant blunders. From the Antoniophone, the Baroxiton, the Bimboniphone (not for children but invented by a G Bimboni, *c* 1850), the Dog Horn, the Herculesophone (very big and powerful), the Highamphone (inventor Mr Higham) to the Psalmelodicon (for church bands?). The Hell Horn, patented in 1843 by a German, Ferdinand Hell, sounds like a counterblast to the Last Trump, for people going in the opposite direction, but unfortunately sounds more hellish in English than German: to have the same frightening effect in that language it would have to be called *Höllenhorn*.

On the other hand, the Irish Helicon, or Hibernicon, suggests something like an Irish musical joke. But it was a real instrument, invented and patented in 1823 by the Reverend Joseph R Cotter, vicar of Castlemagner, County Cork – a giant bass horn which, an enraptured critic said when he heard it at the York Festival in 1835, 'like Goliath it towered heavenwards … such is the power of this Hibernicon that trumpets at the walls of Jericho, nay, the last trump itself, would be as child's play to it.' It was built for Mr Cotter by the aptly named Thomas Key, who added woodwind-like keys to brass instruments, and thus invented the Keyed Bugle – for whose Austrian cousin, built by Anton Weidinger, Haydn's and Hummel's Trumpet Concertos were written.

Mr Pot reinvents notation

Western musical notation as we know it, the system of semibreves, minims, crotchets and quavers, arranged on, above and below the five-line stave and modified by sharps and flats, is not perfect but it has taken a thousand years to evolve and has served composers and performers from the Abbess Hildegard of Bingen to Baron Britten of Aldeburgh. Twentieth-century avant-gardists have experimented with squiggles, blobs, graphs and wiring-diagrams ('graphic notation') which merely disguises the fact that they have nothing comprehensible to say. But would-be reformers occasionally surface who think they can improve the existing system. Most seem to have their origins in the difficulties they themselves experienced with the small staff notation, finding it troublesome to learn. Some even combined notes with letters identifying their names (C, D, E, etc, with conventional stems and tails added). All sooner or later disappeared, leaving barely a ripple. Even Tonic Sol-Fa (doh, ray, me, fah, soh, etc), introduced in 1850 by the Reverend John Curwen for singing teaching, failed to have any real influence on serious music.

One system did make a few waves – but only because it was backed by a rich man's fortune – and it, too, sank almost without trace; except that the flotsam is still being washed up, for the simple reason that there was so much of it. It was called Klavarskribo, invented in 1931 by Cornelius Pot, an immensely rich Dutchman (who must have scooped some kind of lottery jackpot) and was meant to be a 'rational' method of piano notation. He founded the Klavarskribo Institute to promote it but, as usual, nobody wanted to know. Yet by 1950 he had issued at his own expense some 10,000 works of the piano repertoire transcribed into Klavarskribo notation. Every browser in second-hand music shops has come across discarded copies but I have yet to meet a pianist who can read it.

Advice from the agony uncles of the Victorian musical press

Readers often sent requests for information to papers like *The Musical Times*, *The Strad*, *The Organist and Choirmaster* and *The Violin Times*. Sometimes they also enclosed compositions – not for publication but expert evaluation and, they doubtless hoped, for a little praise. Such requests were submitted under pseudonyms, perhaps wisely. The replies were sometimes surprisingly snappy and the praise was sparse:

> To Guido: The Hymn is free from positive grammatical errors; and shows a musical feeling which should be diligently cultivated. It is a grave mistake, however, to use only the harmonies of A major and F major for eight successive closes.

> To Alto: Better consult a qualified teacher of singing.

> To Eliza R, Bittingstone: We cannot reply to our correspondent's string of trivial questions.

> To a Distressed Organist: Thanks. Letter too long.

23,662. Fiedler, J., and Ulrich, C. Dec. 22.

Reflectors for observing position of mouth in singing.—Relates to an arrangement of reflectors and mirrors whereby the music on a piano &c. is illuminated while the player remains in the shade, and a singer is enabled to observe the position of the mouth during singing practice. In the arrangement shown a telescopic rod pivoted at *f* carries a reflector *l*, which by means of the screws *g*, *k*, *m* and slot *h* may be adjusted to reflect the light from the lamp *o* upon the music *n*, as indicated by the lines *o*, *o*¹, *o*². Similarly two mirrors *p*, *q* may be adjusted by the screw *t* to allow of the singer watching the mouth, as indicated by the lines *o*, *o*³, *o*⁴, *o*⁵, *o*⁶. The mirrors *p* and *q* may be separated, one being mounted on the lamp stand, and other modifications in detail may be made.

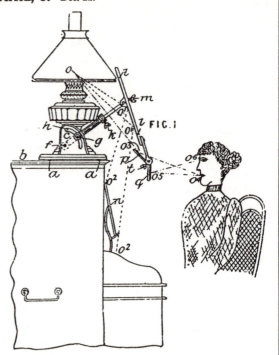

To B flat: See answer to Alto.

To Working Man: The best and cheapest way to learn music and to become an organist is to begin early in life, and to study under the best masters.

To Phyllacardle: Wash it with methylated spirit.

To F E B, Ludlow: Perhaps it would be best to burn it and buy a new one.

Vox: See answer to Alto.

You ask, 'Why the greatest musicians such as Bauer, Pachmann, Godowsky, Paderewski, etc, have no letters to their names.' If your question refers to prefixes, Mr, Miss or Mrs, their being dropped is supposed to show great distinction. If, however, you refer to affixes, we expect it is because they have not passed the necessary examinations. We are unable to say whether they went in and failed. Fools rush in where angels fear to tread.

To A A P: We fear that there is no market among composers of operas for 'a number of melodies, unharmonized', even though they be, as you say, 'undoubtedly original and of considerable value'. Composers of operas have a way of preferring to invent their own melodies, or at least they endeavour to do so; even if, as is sometimes the case, they are not always successful in the attainment of originality. When you are more advanced in the study of harmony, you may be glad to draw from the store which you have already made – perhaps for your Opus 1, even though it may not be an opera.

To Vocalist, Southfields: Your letter is a bit on the incoherent side, but we gather that you won't take our word for it as to Beethoven's never having visited England. You say 'I can assure you that he lived a part of his time in Brook Street, the same as Handel ...' This is as much of your letter as we understand, and it happens to be inaccurate.

To H G F, Kilkenny: We are much obliged for your able and interesting letter, but regret that we are unable to avail ourselves of its contents.

To Dora: We do not know of a pianoforte solo called 'Sweet Peas'. Do you not mean *Suite de pièces*?

5

The land without music

Herr Schmitz hates England – and coins a phrase

It always makes a good, sardonic headline for articles about British composers – 'The land without music' – but I have never seen it correctly attributed. Heinrich Heine, Friedrich Nietzsche, Felix Mendelssohn, Robert Schumann, Hans von Bülow – even the Nazi propaganda minister Joseph Goebbels – have all at some time or other been accused of making this absurdly facile statement.

Das Land ohne Musik is actually the title of a book by Oscar A H Schmitz, published in 1914. The date is significant, for it was written and first published during the time of growing tension between Germany and Britain in the years preceding the First World War which culminated in the German *Gott strafe England* (God punish England) campaign – and, incidentally, Britain's anti-German songs in both World Wars were invariably satirical, whereas the other side produced only hymns of hate. Schmitz's book is in fact not primarily about music but purports to analyse the British character and way of life: politics, snobbery, religion, women, puritanism, sex, suffragettes; British narrow-mindedness (as the author perceived it); the British approach to immigrants – Chinese and Jewish – which he admired for its liberality and tolerance. In a chapter describing his visit to Dublin (Southern Ireland was then part of the United Kingdom and was therefore lumped together by foreigners, with Wales and Scotland, into England), Schmitz compares the Irish character with that of the British – to the detriment of the latter, of course.

Like many polemicists he is a master of the half-truth and wild generalization, often, however, mingled with flashes of acute observations. Music is seldom mentioned. Nevertheless, Part I (Social Problems) is prefaced by an extract from Nietzsche's *Beyond Good and Evil* which sets the tone for Schmitz's own thoughts (and the passage quoted may also account for the subsequent erroneous attribution to Nietzsche of those familiar four words, *Das Land ohne Musik*):

> What offends one, even in the case of the most humane Englishman, is his lack of music. To speak by simile (and, indeed, without): he has no rhythm, no dance, in the movements of his soul and of his body; nay, he even lacks a desire for rhythm and dance; in other words – for 'music'... the English are the only cultured race without a music of their own (music-hall ditties excepted). I say music of their own, for perhaps more foreign music is performed in England than in any other country. That means not only that their ears are less discerning, but that their whole inward life must be poorer. To have music in oneself, and were it but so little, means to possess the faculty of solving what is rigid, of feeling the world as a stream and all events in it as a passing. To have music in oneself means being able to lose oneself, to bear, nay to dwell on, dissonances, because they are dissolvable into harmony. Music lends wings and renders the wonderful intelligible . . .

In Chapter XII (The Stage), Schmitz has this to say:

> That the English are unmusical is known, and one will not be unduly disappointed if the performances at their concerts, save when executed by Continental talent, fall short of our requirements. The English find the approach to music not through the heart, but through sport and the Church. They recognize that it is no mean feat to play a difficult concerto by Beethoven, and they congregate at the performances of those who are considered, for the time being, as the 'champions' of this particular sport. Moreover, they esteem in oratorio music a bit of divine service. At Brighton, once, on a Good Friday, I heard Handel's *Messiah* not very brilliantly performed; the audience were fairly bored, yet it would have been thought bad form to go away before the big Hallélujah. That chorus was listened to standing, but then the hall rapidly emptied itself as

the numbers proceeded; and when not more than a third of the audience were left, the conductor with quick decision cut out the rest and immediately put on the final chorus.

A mass walkout from even the most dire performance of the *Messiah*? Unthinkable. Schmitz probably did not know that it was customary for British performances of Handel's *Messiah* (an oratorio then seldom heard on the Continent) to cut many of the numbers between the Hallélujah Chorus and the final 'Worthy is the Lamb'. Nor would he have known about the royal tradition to rise for its most famous chorus, started by George II at the first London performance on 23 March 1743. But perhaps Schmitz knew that Queen Victoria was really a German (born in England only by the

He: AWFULLY JOLLY CONCERT, WASN'T IT? AWFULLY JOLLY THING BY THAT FELLOW — WHAT'S HIS NAME? — SOMETHING LIKE DOORKNOB.
She: DOORKNOB! WHOM DO YOU MEAN? I ONLY KNOW OF BEETHOVEN, MOZART, WAGNER, HANDEL ...
He: THAT'S IT! HANDEL. I KNEW IT WAS SOMETHING YOU CAUGHT HOLD OF!

(By kind permission of *Punch*)
1898

skin of her teeth) and hated the composer of *The Messiah* ('Handel always tires me,' she said, and left instructions that the Dead March from *Saul* was under no circumstances to be played at her funeral).

Of course, Schmitz lived at a time when Tudor, Elizabethan and Jacobean music were receiving far fewer performances in this country than now (and probably none in Germany); but had he done a little reading in the excellent libraries available to him in England and Germany he would quickly have realized that Britain was no more the 'Land without Music' than it was later to be the 'Land of Hope and Glory'. (One eminent German musician – so eminent I have forgotten his name – admitted the merit of Purcell's Fantasias for strings but claimed that they showed the 'clear influence of Johann Sebastian Bach': which was remarkable, as they were written about five years before Bach's birth.)

Schmitz grudgingly conceded the greatness of Shakespeare but declared that he had survived only because the Germans had (as he put it) 'discovered Shakespeare anew, and translated his works into our modern [German] tongue, [so that] we are the only nation which still stands in a living relationship to Shakespeare at all.' The English, he said, found Shakespeare 'boring' (he was probably quoting a schoolboy he met on his brief visit to the United Kingdom).

After the First World War, *Das Land ohne Musik* was translated into English by Hans Herzl, and published in 1925 by Jarrolds of London under the literally translated title *The land without music*. In his Foreword Herzl reveals that Schmitz also wrote 'a distinguished book' called *French Social Problems* as well as *England's Political Bequest to Germany, through Benjamin Disraeli, Lord Beaconsfield*.

Schmitz, who was born in 1873, was no more and no less than a travel writer; and as travel writers do, he probably spent a few weeks in the countries on which he pontificated. Like many a roving journalist he assumed that things he did not have time to see did not exist (for example, he would hardly have the opportunity to attend many concerts). He lived until 1931, just not long enough to observe what mischief could be done when hostile propaganda disguised itself as research. Herzl's publishers sensed that the book would meet with criticism when presented to an English readership:

> To ask whether the book is pro- or anti-English would be to 'ignore the quest'. Our author's aim is loftier than the making of a catchpenny appeal to any mob whatsoever. He is after the truth, and of that Englishmen need never be afraid. Mr Schmitz, however, is a German, and it cannot but be of interest and concern to a nation, to see itself mirrored on the retina of one, so lately, through force of circumstances, its enemy. Mr Schmitz's truth is pungent, but not bitter. He is an antagonist with whom Englishmen will deem it a privilege to have crossed blades, and a pleasure, now that the fight is over, to shake hands.

Far from taking offence, the English responded in a typically British manner. They simply ignored the book. So few copies were sold that exemplars are now collectors' pieces; and while the catchy title survives, its author has sunk without trace. Perhaps Schmitz, instead of seeking out Heine and Nietzsche for his introductory quotations, should have turned to another great German, Johann Wolfgang von Goethe, who was not only a poet and a philosopher but also a scientist and therefore less given to making sweeping assertions: *Der Mensch verhöhnt was er nicht versteht*, he said. Man derides what he does not understand.

Blunders to the Right

The ceremonial Burning of the Books on 10 May 1933 outside the Berlin Opera was carried out on the personal orders of Adolf Hitler, who early in his life decided that German culture had to be 'cleansed' of all Jewish influence. The books were to be only a beginning – a symbolic preliminary holocaust, a bonfire lighting the way towards pure, untainted Aryan art. It is tempting to imagine that the ceremony was carried out on a spur-of-the-moment order given by an unstable man subject to fits of uncontrollable rage. With his postage-stamp moustache and pasted-down cow-lick he looked an idiot and, in his high-pitched, hysterically ranting voice he sounded an idiot – but he was not without intelligence; so the order must have been given during one of his carpet-chewing tempers.

A few moments' reflection would have convinced him of the stupidity of attempting a total arts purge – and of the impossibility of carrying it out. He could have ordered a Nazi university professor – there were plenty – to make a preliminary study of how the Russians had conducted their own artistic purges, for after all, they had a couple of decades' start on the Germans. That professor could have told Hitler about bibliographies, and about references in books to other books, music and writings. For example, a volume about mechanical musical instruments by Albert Protz suddenly became unpublishable because it mentioned Jewish authors. The bibliography therefore had to be amended with the warning, 'Jewish authors are distinguished by an asterisk'. They were indeed distinguished authors, who could not be ignored; yet they could also not be quoted.

From the very beginning of their movement the Nazis tied themselves into all manner of ideological knots from which they could never extricate themselves. Having burnt the books they then had to cook the facts, to ludicrous effect. Yet, such is the age-old German capacity for taking things seriously, such is their dogged determination to plod on to the end, that they never realized what asses officials were making of themselves. Not a flicker of humour ever disfigured the square-jawed face of Nazi officialdom. Banning the music of Jewish composers such as Mendelssohn, Mahler or Meyerbeer was comparatively simple – after all, even the liberal BBC during the 1960s and 1970s banned certain composers and broadcasters – in effect stifling their careers – but these proscriptions were based either on personal grudges or a dislike of composers who were thought to write 'tunes'.

In Germany there must have been some party officials or academics who contemplated the impossibility of a complete artistic *Entjudung* ('dejudaification'), yet were unable, or frightened, to speak out and bring the Gauleiters to their senses.

What threw the Nazi rednecks into total disarray was the need for purging not merely Jewish works but also those which, however obliquely, extolled personal freedom, praised free speech or condemned an oppressive state, even an historical one. Suddenly, numerous dramatic works could no longer be produced without some modification of text or plot. Beethoven's *Egmont* and *Fidelio* were rendered unperformable unless the stories were twisted to suit the Nazi ideology. The most distinguished musicians and learned musicologists uttered the crassest nonsense. Thus, in 1938, the respected Bach scholar Arnold Schering felt able to write, 'The victorious finale of Beethoven's *Fidelio* is a prophecy, a premonition – one might almost say an anticipation – of the emergence of the Reich in the twentieth century'. Memoranda flew back and forth between government departments, from Gauleiter to Reichsminister, from opera intendant to orchestra manager, about what could and what could not be performed. A letter from the chief of Hitler's Chancellery, dated 7 June 1941, addressed to the minister for Science, Education and Enlightenment of the People, reads:

Honoured Party Member Rust!

It is the Führer's wish that in future there shall be no more performances of the drama *William Tell* by Friedrich von Schiller, and that this work is not to be employed as reading material in schools.

Heil Hitler!

(Signed) Dr Lammers

No sooner had this edict been passed than it was discovered that

Beethoven's Choral Symphony, too, was to be approached with caution. The 'Ode to Joy' of the last movement had already been performed separately from the symphony and politicized for the 1936 Olympics (setting a precedent for its later, crude annexation as a Euro-anthem and football hymn). But Schiller's words had to be amended before any performances of the entire work were considered in Nazi Germany. The notorious Governor Frank of Crakow declared the Ode *verboten* in occupied Poland. After all, how could Germans sing Schiller's text about *all* men being brothers, while having to make exceptions for Jews, Poles, Russians, gypsies, homosexuals, the mentally ill or the physically handicapped? Chopin's works (especially the 'Revolutionary Study'), were banned in Poland – until Governor Frank let it be known that exhaustive research had proved beyond doubt that Chopin was not a Pole but of German-Alsatian extraction. Not only Polish composers but also German Freemasons were excluded from the brotherhood of man. In the last year of the war, on 2 October 1944, when the Germans must have had more serious things to occupy them, a Dr Herbert Gerigk wrote anxiously to the Supreme State Office:

> Could you please help in the following matter? Ludwig van Beethoven wrote several letters to the publisher Franz Anton Hoffmeister with the superscription, 'Honoured Brother'. Until now, nothing has been known to suggest that Beethoven was a member of a masonic lodge. Yet this unusual form of address would suggest that he was. Would it be possible for you to enlighten us in this important matter, or perhaps furnish me with an address where I might obtain information about freemasonry in Vienna?
>
> Heil Hitler!
>
> (Signed) Gerigk

Problem piled up upon problem. The chief of the Prussian Theatre Committee sent an urgent memorandum to the splendidly titled Dr Rainer Schlösser:

AT A SMOKING CONCERT

Herr Professor: YOU HAF A REMARGAPLY BOWERFUL FOICE, MY VRENT!
Basso: YES? DO YOU THINK IT WILL FILL ST JAMES'S HALL?
Herr Professor: FILL ST CHAMES'S HALL? ACH, MY VRENT, IT WILL NOT ONLY FILL ST
CHAMES'S HALL – IT WILL EMPTY IT!

(By kind permission of *Punch*)
1887

Very honoured Herr Reichs Dramaturg!

I herewith beg you most courteously to enlighten me whether you have any reservations or misgivings about the libretto of the opera called *Brave Mr Punch and Pretty Annie*.

What worried the theatre chief was that Mr Punch (*Kasperl* in German) was always depicted with an unusually long nose, just like those which Streicher's propaganda organ *Der Stürmer* put on Jews – and surely this could mean only one thing? Fortunately Dr Schlösser was able to offer a satisfactory explanation. He told him that the *Kasperl* figure, like the English Mr Punch, went back to the Italian *commedia dell'arte*, whose chief figure Arlecchino had *always* been depicted with a long nose:

> The text of the opera *Brave Mr Punch and Pretty Annie* is by the well-known, talented poet Herybert Menzel, an old colleague. The libretto is German in the best sense of the word, and utterly beyond reproach.

That was the good news. The bad news was that:

> ... the music is by Ernst Viebig, the son of the justly celebrated German woman-novelist Clara Viebig, whose father, however, is the former publisher Cohn. He is therefore a half-Jew ... and there can thus be no question of any performance of *Brave Mr Punch and Pretty Annie*.

Thus Mr Punch's nose was cleared for performance but the librettist's grandfather was a non-person and therefore *verboten*. It perfectly illustrates a German *Flüsterwitz* (a subversive 'whispered joke' – Britain has never had the need for such a word) current during the Nazi period: Question: 'Who is the most desirable woman in Germany?' Answer: 'An Aryan grandmother.' Two such grandparents were required to make a person acceptable under the Nuremberg Race Laws, and the unfortunate Mr Punch did not qualify. He was in good company. Beethoven's song cycle *An die ferne Geliebte* was disqualified by its words because the texts were by the poet and doctor Alois Jeitteles, a member of Beethoven's circle. The fact that he also happened to be a Jew was of no interest to Beethoven, but it made Jeitteles unmentionable in Nazi Germany. They could hardly ban a Beethoven song cycle, so Jeitteles, too, was turned into a non-person. Concert promoters were ordered to state on programmes that the text was by 'an unknown author'.

When musicologists discovered that Mozart's *'Wiegenlied'* – his ever-popular Cradle Song – was not by him but by another Jew, Bernhard Flies, also a doctor poet, they declared that it had to be called a folk-song arrangement by Mozart (an art form Mozart never consciously used). Hundreds of *Lieder* set by Beethoven, Schubert and their contemporaries to texts of the Jewish poet Heinrich Heine were either suppressed or labelled in concert programmes as 'Anonymous'. Mozart's three great Italian operas, *Il nozze di Figaro, Così fan tutte* and *Don Giovanni* were declared unperformable in the original Italian because the libretti were by the Jew Lorenzo da Ponte. They had to be given in German, without da Ponte's name, thus carrying the implication that the German translator given in the programme was the librettist. Half a century on we can laugh about this nonsense, for after all, no lasting harm was done to the survival of the works, which is more than can be said for the thousands of artists who perished.

However, some works were indeed physically destroyed, so as to suppress evidence inconvenient to Hitler's race theories. In the catalogue of Schubert's works by Otto Erich Deutsch, an Austrian musicologist obliged to flee his country who subsequently worked in Cambridge, is listed a setting of the 92nd Psalm by Schubert which the composer made in the last months of his life. The entry bears a note, 'Autograph lost'. Not lost – destroyed, just like the books outside the Berlin Opera House in May 1933.

After the outbreak of war, British music was added to the proscribed list. Beethoven's 'Battle' Symphony, which quotes both 'God save the King' and the 'Marseillaise', had to be quietly suppressed, and Weber's *Jubel* Overture, a work that ends with the Saxon national anthem (sung in the early nineteenth century to 'God save the King') also became unperformable. A recording made during the Nazi period under Paul van Kempen was clumsily sanitized by the laughable substitution of *'Deutschland über Alles'*. Puccini's opera *Madama Butterfly*, which at first promised to be politically friendly in Axis terms – the action being set in Japan and its music composed by an Italian, and which, furthermore, exposed an American naval officer, Lieutenant Pinkerton, as a dirty rotten swine – disqualified itself by quotations of, and allusions to, 'The Star spangled Banner'. Another problem was posed by the operas and oratorios of George Frederic Handel (or Georg Friedrich Händel, as the Germans always insisted on calling him, though the composer for most of his life looked upon himself as more Anglo than Saxon, anglicized his name and dropped the umlaut). Handel, they discovered, had the tiresome habit of choosing stories and libretti adapted from the Old Testament, like *Athalia*, *Jephtha*, *Belshazzar* and *Judas Maccabaeus*. Such texts had not only to be Germanized but also 'dejewed'. The words of Handel's *Messiah*, which are a mixture of both the Old and the New Testaments, came in for particular attention. In April 1941, Hans Georg Görner wrote an article entitled 'Georg Friedrich Händel and Judaism':

> April 13th marks the 200th anniversary of the first performance of Handel's Oratorio *The Messiah*. The issues at stake are not merely musical or historical, but are a matter of *Weltanschaung* ... We must ask: can a people which has been solemnly charged by God with the historic task of waging war against world Jewry *afford* to be heard singing texts about 'telling good tidings to Zion', or invite 'the Daughters of Jerusalem to rejoice'?

The answer was a resounding *nein*. Even traditional Christian sentiments could be made more meaningful for the Reich by updating words for old-time favourites. In *The People's Book for the*

Winter, Gerhard Pallmann makes certain political and seasonable adjustments to carols likely to be sung by German soldiers to keep their spirits up while they froze to death on the Eastern front:

> *Stille Nacht, heilige Nacht,*
> *Deutschlands Söhne halten Wacht*
> *In den Schützengraben verschneit*
> *liegen wir Mann für Mann bereit,*
> *lauern bei Tag und bei Nacht.*

> Silent Night, Holy Night,
> Earth is still, heavens are bright;
> Sons of Germany, side by side,
> In snowbound trenches must abide,
> Lying in wait by day and night.

As decree followed edict and ban succeeded prohibition, the sheer magnitude of the problem of the 'cleansing' of music made ever greater inroads on the Germans' energies and manpower. But things had gone too far and, instead of quietly dropping the whole lunatic idea, the Nazis diverted valuable national resources to the task, thereby helping to bring their own end a little nearer. After all, this was one task for which slave labour was not suitable. The ears of German youth had to be protected; and wherever the Nazis looked there seemed to lurk Jewish composers and performers; and if they were not Jews they might have been imbued with the poison of Anglo-American or Negro decadence.

Jazz was branded 'nigger-jazz' and banned, except when used for propaganda purposes. What was described as the 'gruesome whining noise' of the saxophone was also about to be banished when Nazi military musicians persuaded the authorities that it was useful for marching bands. It was reprieved. But not before its inventor, the Belgian Adolphe Sax, was declared to have been an Adolf and a German.

The Nazis compiled a series of dictionaries devoted to banned musicians and their works, of which the most comprehensive – and unwittingly entertaining – is the *Lexikon der Juden in der Musik* (Directory of Jewish Music and Musicians), in effect a black list. I give just a few examples of the massacred reputations in the Directory:

Yehudi Menuhin is dismissed with just one word, sarcastically isolated in quotation marks: '*Wunderkind.*' The conductor Otto Klemperer is described as the man 'who turned the Kroll Opera House in Berlin into a Jewish-Marxist Experimental Stage for the Perversion of German Masterworks'. Among the misdeeds listed is a production of Wagner's *Tannhäuser* in which the Venusberg was 'turned into a beer cellar where the Goddess of Love squirmed about like a randy tart' and the Pilgrims were 'ragged *Lumpen* proletarians' dressed as 'a football team wearing motoring caps . . .' – not the Klemperer London knew in the 1960s and 1970s. The violinist Fritz Kreisler is mentioned not as the greatest violinist of his time but solely in connection with his famous 'forgeries', and a whole column condemning 'the Jewish violinist' Joseph Joachim manages to avoid mentioning his fruitful artistic relationship and collaboration with Brahms.

Among conductors who blundered into overt support for the Nazis were Karl Böhm, Hans Swarowsky and, most notably, Herbert von Karajan, who claimed that he had joined the Nazi party only because he had to, to obtain his first important post at Aachen (after all, did not Gustav Mahler adopt the Catholic faith because he could otherwise not have been *Generalmusikdirektor* of the Vienna State Opera?). But Karajan lied. Researchers discovered that his Nazi membership card was issued to him when the party was still a proscribed organization, in other words he was a closet Nazi who only came out when it was safe to do so. With a little hindsight it was an understandable thing to do for ambitious conductors, who would sell their grannies to get a rostrum of their own. On the whole only those musicians whose reputation was already established, like Paul Hindemith and the Busch brothers, were prepared to make a stand – or a half-hearted stand, like

Richard Strauss and Wilhelm Furtwängler. The younger ones with unfulfilled ambitions either made compromises or threw themselves wholeheartedly behind the Führer.

It is difficult to believe now that the Nazi nightmare lasted only (if one can use that word) a dozen years. But the Nazis' *Kulturgauleiter* (a contrived but precisely descriptive term) continued to operate with unabated fanaticism even while the ragged remains of German armies were shambling towards prison camps with hands raised in surrender ...

Blunders to the Left

When the Nazis took power in Germany they could to some extent look to the Soviet experience of how to manipulate the arts and cleanse them of supposedly hostile influences and politically incorrect material. The Romanovs had hardly been models of humanity and tolerance, but under their rule musicians were able to compose and perform more or less what they wished, so long as it did not offend the court. The traditionally incompetent Russian bureaucracy would have made central control all but impossible. If only for this reason the post-1917 Soviets committed fewer blunders than the Nazis were to do, with their Germanic zeal and Teutonic thoroughness.

In Tsarist Russia composition had been largely in the hands of the aristocracy and the middle classes, and was therefore foreign dominated: even Jewish artists and intellectuals could ply their trade in the face of ruthless imperial repression of minorities: pogroms were for the poor.

When the Revolution had been accomplished Lenin clearly stated that creative freedom and individuality of expression were the lifeblood of Soviet art and artists, so under his inspiration the revolutionaries concentrated, first, on the establishment of a network of well-organized conservatories, opera studios and other teaching institutions. It was a wise and prescient decision, and laid the foundation of later Soviet excellence among performers. Many of the artists who benefited were Jews, as indeed many of the early revolutionary Communists had been, because they had even more reason to fight for the overthrow of the tsars than Christian Russians.

Sovietization, state control and nationalization of music publishing soon followed, and were accomplished without too many blunders: the progressive outside world saw the revolutionaries as idealists, and fervently wanted them to succeed, so it would generally refrain from holding up to ridicule the odd artistic blunder committed by over-zealous new brooms. Only when the ignorant party rednecks entered the fray did artistic repression begin to bite.

On 29 October 1920, a Party Resolution instituted centralized state control of the arts. It was meant to reflect 'universal Socialist thinking' and bring a 'high ideo-revolutionary quality to all artistic production'. Nevertheless, free-thinking composers continued to go their own way – and did so without serious sanctions. Even after six years of Communism, in 1923, Soviet composers were able to form an Association for Contemporary Music, whose concerts in Leningrad were permitted to feature avant-garde works by Berg, Schönberg and Stravinsky. In the same year, however, the infighting began, with the founding of the worker-based Russian Association of Proletarian Musicians, which aimed to speed up 'the proletarianization of culture', or 'Proletkult' (as true Socialist pioneers they took a delight in inventing idiotic acronyms, just as would-be social manipulators do today). In the tradition of the brotherly strife that follows all successful revolutions, the liberal, long-haired progressives of the ACM fought bitter battles with the shaven-headed philistines of the RAPM. Nevertheless, the two factions co-existed in an uneasy peace for several years: arguments were verbal and restrained and neither felt the need to shout down the others' concerts with carefully staged protests, a practice the Nazis were soon to turn into a fine art.

Then, in 1932, when the squabbling threatened to get out of hand, the Central Committee of the Communist Party peremptorily dissolved both factions and replaced them with a single Union of Soviet Composers, under the rigid control of the Kremlin. This USC was to regulate all musical endeavour for its own narrow political ends until the very end of Communism, and it was during this period that the worst blunders were committed. Strict rules were laid down which Soviet composers were obliged to follow, as to what kind of music they were to write. The works had to be direct, easily understood, optimistic and rousing – in a word, Socialist. The USC ruled that the use of folk song and dance was to be encouraged, while 'modernism' of any kind was banned. Very quickly Russian musicians became isolated from the music that was being produced by the rest of the world. They were largely kept in ignorance of it – shielded not only from the works of Russian emigré composers, like Stravinsky and the early Prokofiev (who were particularly reviled, as revisionist traitors), but also from the serialists of the Second Viennese School, the approachable music of anti-Nazi Germans like Hindemith, as well as the clumping earthiness of Carl Orff (whose music received the seal of personal approval of Adolf Hitler). Even the works of good German Communists like the exiled Kurt Weill and his pupils were declared alien and decadent, but perhaps most hateful of all to the Soviets were the Gallic frivolities of Les Six. The cheerful confections emanating from Nadia's *boulangerie* were declared neo-bourgeois anathema to Soviet-Socialist principles.*

The commissars understood well enough that artists reacted better to the carrot than the stick, and those who produced sycophantic Odes to Stalin, giant Stakhanovite Symphonies, Workers' Choruses, or Cantatas in Memory of Lenin, found themselves generously rewarded with money, dachas and privileges. There was a lucrative industry in the setting-to-music

*Nadia Boulanger (1887-1979), internationally renowned teacher of Aaron Copland, Jean Françaix, Lennox Berkeley, Igor Markevich, Walter Piston and many others.

of all the turgid, cliché-ridden speeches of their masters. Compositions had to pass the Stalin Test. If the low-browed Georgian peasant understood it, it was pronounced good. To this end Stalin appointed a personal arts adjutant, Andrei Zhdanov, a kind of musical equivalent of the tsars' food taster, to make sure his master's ears were not being poisoned: it was Zhdanov who determined the degree of wholesomeness and 'Socialist Realism' of new works, as well as investigating their creators' political probity. Melodic simplicity and patriotic uplift, and above all optimism, became the yardsticks by which works of Soviet art were measured. Corruption was rife, not only financial but also linguistic. The tendentious Soviet vocabulary lost little in translation when transformed into absurdly stilted English which branded dissenters as 'lackeys of the west', 'revisionist running dogs' or 'capitalist hyenas'. The greatest crime (undefined because undefinable) a composer could commit was that of 'bourgeois western formalism'. Shostakovich was a notable victim, and in 1936 his satirical *Lady Macbeth of Mtsenk* led to a kind of artistic show trial which reviled him as 'a tool of capitalist music': capitalist tools always figured large in the propaganda vocabulary.

Yet conservatoires and music schools continued to be run on the hothouse/powerhouse principles applied to the training of athletes and ballet dancers, and turned out world-class musical performers as if on a production line. The state always made special provision for ultra-gifted performers. After the Second World War hundreds of Soviet artists were sent to tour the western world, providing the state with hard currency – and the artists and even some of the commissars themselves with useful contacts for eventual defection. It was joked that when the Leningrad String Orchestra toured in the west it returned home as the Leningrad String Trio.

After 1968 the official bans on works or composers were eased, but those musicians who were regarded as the most patriotic (and the least discordant) tended to get state commissions, decorations and subsidies. Shostakovich, earlier condemned as a 'formalist', had by this time been grudgingly rehabilitated, partly because he went through the motions of a grovelling recantation and partly because his music sold well in the west, bringing royalties in foreign currency. While still giving his works patriotic titles, Shostakovich was now able to write the kind of music he liked to write. Some dissident composers embraced western serialism with a vengeance – not because they liked it but because it gave them the means of showing two fingers to the commissars who loathed it. By the same token these composers raised their own stock in the west, because conductors, performers and musical entrepreneurs considered it their duty to play the dissidents' music.

After many of his works were banned as being 'tainted with formalist perversions', Prokofiev good-naturedly defined

Soulful Man (as the orchestra plays): BEETHOVEN CAN'T TOUCH TCHAIKOVSKY.
Stranger: I DESSAY. SOME THINGS DISAGREE WITH ME.

(By kind permission of *Punch*)
1929

formalism as 'music people don't understand at first hearing'. After the 1917 Revolution many musicians and composers who fled the new regime settled in the west, among them Stravinsky, Koussevitzky, Rachmaninov, Medtner, the two Tcherepnins and Prokofiev. Some tentatively or briefly returned to the fold (Russians are always prone to weep into their drink with exaggerated love for their mother country) only to meet with mixed fortunes. Prokofiev was among several who fell foul of Zhdanov and was reviled with strictures and denunciations of 'formalism', the old standby swear-word. Yet none, to my knowledge, was actually persecuted or exiled to Siberia (as were dissident writers or scientists). They were merely deprived of their livelihood. Much of the irony in Prokofiev's music can be interpreted as attempts to discredit his ignorant critics and his final, if inadvertent, act of irony was to die on the same day as Stalin, after which his proscribed works were gradually unbanned.

During the Stalin years numerous idiotic blunders were committed. Puccini's *Tosca* became unperformable, because it reflected badly on that sacred Communist cow, officialdom. It was therefore fitted with a new story and libretto and was renamed *The Battle for the Commune*. Glinka's *A Life for the Tsar* was too valuable a work to be discarded as it is by the father of modern Russian music, so it was not only de-tsarified but rewritten as *The Hammer and Sickle*. Tchaikovsky's '1812' Overture posed a problem, as it contained towards the end a triumphant, fortissimo quotation of the old tsarist Russian anthem, a tune banned on pain of death. A Soviet composer (whose name was apparently not divulged) set to work and substituted another tune, a jaunty bit of neo-Glinka. It fits neither harmonically nor melodically, but the commissars were happy. Not only was any mention of Tchaikovsky's homosexuality forbidden but that poignant suicide note, his Symphony No 6 in B minor, was turned inside out to end not with the slow, despairing epilogue but with the March, in keeping with Socialist optimism.

British followers of the Communist party line were by and large untouched by such dialectic excesses, especially after the exposure of Stalinism and the occupation of Hungary and Czechoslovakia. Only two English composers followed anything like a strict Communist party line. Cornelius Cardew, whose compositions were usually not music at all but games in which anyone could take part, without bothering to learn any musical skills.*

Alan Bush (1900-95) remained an unreconstructed Communist to the end of his life, even beyond the end of Communism itself. He was an accomplished composer and a delightful conversationalist, yet he had a political blind spot. So seriously did he take Stalin's call for Socialist optimism that he banished from his musical vocabulary the interval of a falling semitone, as is exemplified in the centuries-old 'appoggiatura', a sigh or dying fall, eg, a C followed by the B immediately below it. Most of Bush's works had 'workerist' themes, like *Wat Tyler*, a children's opera on the life of a medieval English rebel, *The Sugar Reapers*, *The Ballad of Aldermaston* (the scene of anti-nuclear protests in the 1960s and 1970s – surely an 'Aldermaston March' would have been more apt?), *Songs of Asian Struggle*, etc. If there was a miners' strike somewhere, Bush was sure to set it to music. As a result he occupied a unique position in European music: to the East Germans he was the best-known of all English composers, and they nearly always had one or other of his operas in the repertoire; while he remained practically unknown in Britain: no doubt a bit of judicious Radio 3 black listing helped. In earlier days he and the poet, Randall Swingler, updated at least one Handel opera with Marxist, anti-capitalist and anti-imperialist words, so that where Handel's *Belshazzar* had:

> All Empires upon God depend,
> Begun by His command, at His command they end:

*An orchestra embracing Cornelius Cardew's musical philosophy, the Portsmouth Sinfonia, briefly came to national notice in the 1970s and made a few excruciating recordings which for a time enjoyed cult status. The orchestra was open to all comers, held no auditions, and the sole condition for entry was that members brought an instrument they were unable to play. Indeed, any member found practising was instantly dismissed.

> Look up to Him in all your ways:
> Begin with Pray'r, and end with Praise ...

Bush and Swingler's London Co-operative Workers' Chorus sang:

> All Empires upon force depend,
> Begun by greed's command, at man's command they end:
> And those who make oppression cease
> Begin with war but end in peace.

In Communist Poland composers suffered less interference from government bureaucracy, but Polish artists who formed too close ties with their western colleagues were disapproved of. Henryk Górecki provides a good example of the pull between Communist forces and western influence. He started his career as a kind of Polish Vaughan Williams, writing folksy and passionately traditional music (what in England is known as the Cowpat School), works which ordinary people could not only understand but sing and play. And a good thing too. But when the young Górecki became politically aware and felt threatened by the commissars, he embraced the teachings of Theodor Adorno: not in a dialectical sense but because discordant and unapproachable music was not liked by the Communists. He wrote dense, post-Schönbergian serialist music, which won the approbation of earnest western intellectuals and gained him international prizes; in other words, performances and dollars. With a number of other pro-western Polish avant gardists he was regarded in the west as a shining light against East-European artistic repression, second only to Pyotr Zak.

Came the fall of Communism – coinciding neatly with that of serialism – and Górecki once more trimmed his creative sails to the changed wind. This time it was blowing from the United States, where the new minimalists like Steve Reich, John Adams, Philip Glass and Terry Riley had carved out a lucrative niche for themselves, using minimal talents and minuscule physical effort to gain maximum royalties. They also inspired a few feeble British imitators, who gained some success through the infallible over-exposure by film background music.

The wheel of fortune is constantly turning, and the New Minimalism became a new kind of exploitation of workers by capitalists. Minimalism took the sweat out of composing and put it where it belonged, on the brows of the performers, the workers, who were required slavishly and endlessly to repeat simple diatonic fragments, and often cleverly weave them into shifting patterns, which requires enormous stamina. Once again the back-breaking effort fell on the workers, who had to play repetitive music for hours on end, while the capitalist composers laughed all the way to the bank. For the first time in musical history it became possible to compose music faster than the time it took to perform it.

The authorities are frightened of musicians

It was understandable that the Israel Philharmonic never invited Herbert von Karajan or Karl Böhm to conduct, as both had been staunch Nazis. But their ban of the music of Wagner, a proto-Nazi long dead even before Hitler came on the scene, has been widely condemned as absurd. The Gilbert and Sullivan operetta *The Mikado* is still banned in Japan because it treats their emperor in a faintly undignified light; and Muslim countries have an aversion to Mozart's *Die Entführung aus dem Serail*, because it contains some mild banter about the Prophet (although it has never really been a problem, as Mozart opera performances in Arab countries could be counted on the fingers of a convicted shoplifter's hand).

The truth is that artistic censorship always makes the censors look foolish. Until recently England, too, had an artistic censor, the Lord Chamberlain, an office going back to Tudor times, when

Henry VII appointed a Master of the King's Revels and Licenser of Plays. His task was to ensure that performances of music and drama did not contain anything (in word, deed or dress) that was offensive to the king and, by implication, to his subjects at large. His other duties included the emptying of royal chamberpots – quaint and archaic offices, like those of the Ladies of the Royal Bedchamber and the Master of the Royal Piggeries.

With the passing of years the Lord Chamberlain became more liberal but (as the Theatres Act 1843 laid down) he still kept an eye on 'every tragedy comedy farce opera burletta interlude melodrama pantomime and other entertainment of the stage or any part thereof'. When a London newspaper wrote in 1875, 'The Lord Chamberlain lengthened the skirts of the ballet', readers knew that he did not personally wield needle-and-thread to cover the young women's knees. Lords Chamberlain were ridiculed for seeing lewdness or obscenity where none was intended and some, on retirement, revealed that they had uncommonly dirty minds. He wielded his 'blue pencil' until after the Second World War (when that implement of censorship performed its national service, though in fact the official censor used a red one). Only the Theatres Act 1968 put an end to such nonsense.

Opera was usually left alone, with preliminary inspections of the libretti but by and large ignoring later interpolations (about which he was very keen in the theatre). The officers probably knew that most of the sung words would be inaudible anyway, and that composers and librettists, like W S Gilbert and Sir Arthur Sullivan, had a shrewd idea what they could safely lampoon. Their satires against MPs, the House of Lords, the British army and (suitably disguised) royalty itself, never got them into serious trouble. Foreigners, however, had to tread warily when they brought their productions to London. For example, the Lord Chamberlain's regulations concerning the depiction of biblical characters on stage prevented Saint-Saëns's *Samson and Delilah* from being seen by English audiences during almost the entire first century of its existence. Before 1968 musicals like *Jesus Christ Superstar*, *Godspell* or *Joseph and his Amazing Technicolour Dreamcoat* would have been out of the question, and *Hair* unthinkable.

Elsewhere in Europe and beyond, a profusion of royal and political prohibitions made the English censor's strictures look mild by comparison. Verdi's opera of 1859, *Un ballo in maschera*, to Scribe's libretto, was based on the assassination in 1792 of King Gustav of Sweden. But the depiction of regicide, even by way of an operatic fantasy, was strictly *verboten* in every monarchy, so the plot was changed to make the victim English: the governor of Boston, Mass, USA – still a fantasy, as there was no such post even when the British ruled North America.

Verdi's *Giovanna d'Arco* incurred a different kind of state disapproval in France. In the libretto, by Solera after Schiller, Joan of Arc fights the English after falling in love with the Dauphin. She dies in his arms as he succeeds to the throne as Charles VII. The French authorities did not approve of this wilful falsification of history: Joan, as every schoolboy knew, was burnt at the stake. But no nineteenth-century stage lighting could have effectively represented a burning at the stake and, even without such tricks, opera houses and theatres regularly burnt to the ground. Verdi therefore had to have her shot by a firing squad. Another of his operas, *Un giorno di regno* (King for a Day, literally, A Day of Reign) concerns King Stanislaw of Poland but otherwise incurred no disapproval (though the imaginative translation of its title as 'A Rainy Day' gave a rather different idea of the plot).

In the early nineteenth century, when the novels of Sir Walter Scott became popular all over Europe, it was fashionable for Italian composers to hire librettists to adapt Scott's novels for them, or else provide them with cheaper imitations, usually concerning wonderful, romantic-sounding places in Scotland and northern England. That is why there were operas like *Lucia di Lammermoor*, *La Prigione di Edimburgo* (the Siege of Edinburgh), *Le Brasseur de Preston* (The Brewer of Preston) and (a little further south) *Il Castello di Kenilworth*, to name only a few.

In 1824 Donizetti composed the most ludicrous 'English' opera of all – the splendidly named *Emilia di Liverpool*. The story is far-fetched even by normal operatic standards (and I know about this one because I rediscovered it in the 1950s and produced a concert performance, when it provided the young Joan Sutherland with her first Donizetti role). Liverpool, we are told, is 'situated in a beautiful alpine landscape not many leagues distant from London'. Emilia, the daughter of a noble Scouser called Claudio di Liverpool, has been seduced and abandoned by a faithless lover. As a consequence, her mother – unable to come to terms with the idea of Emilia turning into a single-parent family – dies of shame. To add to the family misfortunes, Claudio, her father, is convicted of some unnamed political crime and condemned to 20 years' slavery in Africa (an interesting reversal of practice of the time, when slaves were still travelling in the opposite direction); though in another version he is himself a Liverpool sea captain in the West India Trade (the euphemism for the transportation of African slaves).

One aspect of Donizetti's Liverpool does have an authentic ring, and that is the weather, which is dreadful. Indeed *Emilia di Liverpool* opens with a thunderstorm which – and this is another absurd operatic tradition – is of positively tropical duration, precisely 24 bars before the sun comes out again. In its aftermath, three foreign travellers are found in the swirling waters of the Mersey, into which their coach has overturned. They are rescued by the chorus – described as a band of 'Liverpool Mountaineers' – and brought to dry out in a hospice on the mountaintop outside Liverpool (somewhere round Mossley Hill, overlooking Woolton, one would guess). When the mishap occurred the travellers had been on their way from Italy to London, via Liverpool (Donizetti's and his librettist Giuseppe Checcherini's geography was even hazier than their history). They were Asdrubale, a Neapolitan count; his niece, Bettina; and one Colonello Villars, who is travelling, heavily disguised *sotto nome di Tompson* – under the name of Tompson (without an *h*). Light relief is provided by Don Romualdo, who sings throughout in a thick Neapolitan dialect – Italy's equivalent of Scouse. Milordo Tompson (also called 'Sir

Tompson' for short) is none other than the wicked seducer. After all those years he is searching for Emilia, to ask her forgiveness. And who should be running that hospice on the mountaintop outside Liverpool but Emilia herself ... It is all good stuff for revenge arias, duels, recognition scenes, and in the end, a grand reconciliation. Even old Claudio is let out on parole (or, in another version, escapes from Africa) and arrives home just in time.

One can never take it for granted that the weather will be right *outside* the opera house, either. In one of the Welsh National Opera productions of Verdi's *Aida*, at the place in the opera where the Egyptian armies march through the desert, the custom is that the legions – in reality the men of the chorus – march across the stage, then behind the backdrop and back on to the stage – round and round to give an impression of huge battalions passing by. In a small Welsh theatre there was simply no room behind the scenery, so the Egyptian legions had to go out through one door at the back of the hall, walk along the street and re-enter by the door at the other side. Unfortunately, whenever it poured with rain the Egyptian soldiers, as they marched across the stage, looked more and more soggy at each circuit, water dripping from their vizors under the burning Egyptian sun. Puccini's *Manon Lascaut*, also set in a sun-parched, desolate place, suffered a related weather disaster but from within the opera house. In Act 4, where the heroine is dying of thirst 'in a vast desert near the outskirts of New Orleans', just as she was singing her final aria, '*Sola, perduta, abbandonata*', a careless stagehand pulled the wrong lever and released a polystyrene snowstorm that was ready up in the flies for the first act of *La Bohème* the following night. And incidentally, the geographical setting in this opera, too, is open to question. There are, of course, no deserts on the 'outskirts of New Orleans' and no one is likely to die of thirst, though there is a considerable risk of one's sinking into a swamp and being eaten by alligators.

Mrs and Mrs Finke love Fidelio

The German composer Fidelio Finke (1891-1968) came from a notable family of Czech musicians which also produced Smetana's teacher and exerted a lasting influence on the teaching of music in that most musical of provinces. The Finkes were rooted in Bohemia but felt German at heart (the name means Finch in German), so when in 1938 Hitler marched into the Sudetenland, the Finkes chirped louder than anyone in welcoming his troops, calling the Führer 'Liberator of Bohemia'. Fidelio Finke served Hitler well, who showered him with honours and commissions, via the notorious Deputy Gestapo Chief, Reinhard Heydrich, 'Protector' of Czechoslovakia. Like other Nazi composers Finke was quickly rehabilitated after the war and allowed to return to work. Both *Grove* and its German equivalent *Musik in Geschichte und Gegenwart* gave him sanitized biographies. Both unaccountably forgot to mention Finke's wartime output, though the latter is at pains to say that Finke dedicated his String Quartet of 1914 to Arnold Schönberg – notice that such homage to a Jewish composer, which a few decades later would have tainted him, was now used as whitewash. Both dictionaries omit Finke's 50-minute-long 'German Cantata' for the Nazis, and his 'Hymn to the Liberation of Bohemia' from their detailed work lists.

Finke is now remembered chiefly for his family's obsession with stage characters (his uncle was Romeo Finke, also a Sudeten Czech musician) and especially with Beethoven's 'Liberation' opera *Fidelio* (though what Beethoven had in mind was liberation from, not by, tyranny). Old Mr and Mrs Finke produced a large brood, of whom Fidelio Finke was the eldest. He was followed by Leonore Finke, Marzelline Finke, Rocco, Jacquino, Pizzarro and so on, all the way down the opera's cast list. They thought that Mrs Finke had finished childbearing when, late in their marriage, she unexpectedly gave birth to twins. These they called First Prisoner and Second Prisoner.

Oh, I'm glad you've got a piano in the rooms. What is it? A Broadwood?
No, mum. Myogh'ny!

(By kind permission of *Punch*)
1895

Feminists don't care for Beethoven

Any female music lover afraid of getting herself into what is now called 'a rape-conducive environment' (such as is now found by some in every office, orchestra or cocktail party), would do well:

> ... to read Henry Beard and Christopher Cerf's *Sex and Dating*. This warns, for example, that if you wish to show solidarity with the anti-rape movement it is unwise to invite a girl to a performance of Beethoven's Ninth Symphony. Feminist musicologist Susan McClary of the University of Minnesota has pointed out that this 'contains one of the most horrifying moments in music', the persistent repetition of a phrase until it 'finally explodes in the throttling murderous rage of a rapist'.

Independent on Sunday,
1994

Ruskin patronizes young women

In music especially you will soon find what personal benefit there is in being serviceable: it is probable that, however limited your powers, you have voice and ear enough to sustain a note of moderate compass in a concerted piece – that, then, is the first thing to make sure you can do. Get your voice disciplined and clear, and think only of accuracy; never of effect or expression: if you have any soul worth expressing, it will show itself in your singing; but most likely there are very few feelings in you, at present, needing any particular expression; and the one thing you have to do is to make a clear-voiced little instrument of yourself, which other people can entirely depend upon for the note wanted.

From *Sesame and Lilies*, John Ruskin, 1819-1900

The Huddersfield Choral Society fears Socialists

During the 1880s, after the passing of the Education Act, Liverpool attempted to enforce school attendance with an ingenious scheme for flushing out truants. Itinerant musicians were cheap – usually German Oom-Pah Bands, economic migrants as they would now be called – whom the corporation hired to play on street corners during the day, when children should have been at school. As soon as a band struck up, children would run from their houses, straight into the arms of school inspectors lurking behind the big drum.

The Huddersfield Choral Society, which was formed in 1836 and is still the most famous choir in the north of England, also used music for some gentle social engineering in an attempt to improve the lot of the working classes. A healthy and happy worker was an efficient one, but mill owners were losing the battle against gin palaces. Successive Truck Acts put obstacles in the way of paying workers in non-currency tokens (which were exchangeable at company-owned shops for food and essentials but invalid in public houses), so the employers progressed from brass tokens to brass bands, luring the men with attractive uniforms and free refreshment at band practice. Better still, they bought them their instruments, in the belief that music can tame not only wild beasts but also the British working man. To get the women involved (and in those days female brass players were unthinkable) the mill owners founded choral societies – some eight years before the arrival from Germany of Joseph Mainzer and his Singing for the Million movement, usually credited with the founding of the nineteenth-century British choral tradition. Provision was made for instrumentalists as well as singers to take part, and meetings were held weekly, monthly and quarterly, presumably working up towards performances.

In 1842 the Huddersfield Choral Society revised its rules with special regard to the dangers of the emerging Socialist movement. In addition, the famous blunt speaking of the Yorkshireman had to be curbed, with the threat of a half-crown fine. Here is a selection from the Rule Book:

Rule II That meetings shall be held on the Friday on or before the full moon of every month.

Rule IX That on the Monthly nights each member shall be allowed three gills of ale, bread, cheese, etc, and on the Quarterly, such other refreshments as shall be agreed upon by the Committee.

Rule XIII Should any member or members leave the Orchestra before the conclusion of any performance, without giving a satisfactory reason to the Leader, he or she shall be fined sixpence.

Rule XXI That at the monthly meetings any member shall be allowed to give his or her opinion on any piece of music, provided it be done in a respectful, friendly and becoming manner; but not to stop, interrupt, or make any disturbance ... on pain of forfeiting the sum of two shillings and sixpence for each offence, or be excluded.

Rule XXII Any member being intoxicated, or using obscene or abusive language shall forfeit sixpence for each offence.

Rule XXVI That any member taking a copy away without first acquainting the Librarian shall be fined two shillings and sixpence.

Rule XXVIII That no person shall be a member of this Society who frequents the 'Hall of Science' or any of the 'Socialist Meetings'; nor shall the Librarian be allowed to lend (knowingly) any copies of music belonging to this Society to any Socialists, upon pain of expulsion.

The employers were terrified of 'Socialists', as the word was then quite new, defined in 1833 as one '... who preaches of community of goods, abolition of crime, of punishment, of magistrates, and of marriage'. The Halls of Science were the brainchild of the Welsh social reformer Robert Owen (1771-1858), whose Owenism frightened the employers almost as much as Socialism and Communism, then also known as 'Communionism'.

6

The Lost Chord

Seated one day at the organ,
I was anxious and ill at ease,
For I found upon inspection,
There were several missing keys.
I knew not what I was playing
(Though 'twas hymn two hundred and ten),
But it made a row like a starving cow
When it came to the grand 'Amen'.

I sought to discover the meaning
Of a sound so wide and weird;
I crept inside on hands and knees
And found just what I had feared.
The flute and the vox humana
Were mute and declined to sing:
The reeds, alack, showed many a crack
And I tied them up with string.

The bellows I neatly mended
With a blower's trouser-brace;
I managed well to secure the swell
With a stamp and an old boot-lace.
But I'd made my efforts vainly,
I lost my temper then,
And said a word which the parson heard –
And was not a grand 'Amen'.

Magazine of the Sheffield and District
Organists' and Choirmasters' Association, 1994

Mrs Procter gets lost among the chords

When Mrs Adelaide Procter (1825-64) in her *Legends and Lyrics*, a collection of poems written between 1858 and 1861, mislaid 'The Lost Chord', she could hardly have foreseen that its banal opening 'Seated one day at the organ/I was weary and ill at ease ...' would one day enter the language to become one of the best-known lines in English. It has long been the favourite religious song after 'Abide with Me' and inspired dozens of wicked parodies. Sir Arthur Sullivan (normally a most fastidious composer) did not exactly help by setting the first 13 syllables to a single note, which he drearily repeats 13 times – right up to 'ill at ease', when, almost reluctantly, the tune moves up a note. As an organist of the time said, 'It is very difficult in these days to be original, for if you repeat the note F a certain number of times with a particular rhythm, you plagiarize 'The Lost Chord'.

The text, too, reveals faults almost immediately, with 'And my fingers wander'd idly /Over the noisy keys'. Mrs Procter knew that an organ, unlike a piano, *can* be noisy even when the player's fingers are merely idling: if there is no wind entering the pipes they gently clatter up and down, like mice doing a tap dance, though musically, of course, the keys themselves are noiseless. To make the piece noisy she would first have had to pull out the loudest stops, which no Victorian organist of sound mind would have done when the intention was merely to 'wander idly' over the keyboard. No, she put 'noisy' in front of 'keys' only because she could not think of a better word to fill the scansion. 'Ivory', contracted to 'iv'ry', would have done (though its use on keyboard instruments is now strictly *verboten* for ecological reasons).

'It linked all perplex'd meanings/Into one perfect peace' scans only if one uses the archaic stressing, '*perplex'd*'. My copy lamely tries to put this right by using three syllables for three notes, per*plexèd*: in Victorian days composers' and authors' copyrights were not always treated with complete respect.

Most absurd of all is 'I know not what I was playing/Or what I was dreaming then/But I struck one chord of music/like the sound of a great Amen'. Oh, Mrs Procter. *One* chord does not an Amen make, not even in a dream. *Two* will do at a pinch but that is the absolute minimum, producing the familiar, perfunctory Amen cadence IV-I, subdominant-to-tonic, sequence. But I would recommend the Threefold Amen, which is also known as the Dresden Amen because it was first used in that city in the eighteenth century by J G Naumann. Sir John (Crucifixion) Stainer went four better than the Dresden Amen with his Sevenfold Amen, composed for St Paul's Cathedral. Such far-from-lost chords can be heard in Wagner's *Parsifal*, Mendelssohn's 'Reformation' Symphony and works by Bruckner and Stanford. But a one-chord Amen – impossible.

As for the religious feelings expressed in the song, they turn out to be humbug. Sullivan wrote the music for Mrs Fanny Ronalde, the wife of a complaisant and rich American and Sullivan's long-term mistress, whom he installed in a convenient London apartment. The manuscript of 'The Lost Chord' was long ago declared lost, but it was subsequently claimed that Mrs Ronalde had instructed that after her death it should be buried with her, the music placed in the coffin across her breast. If the story is true – and Arthur Jacobs, Sullivan's biographer, who knows more about his life than any other person, throws doubt on it – 'The Lost Chord' is not so much lost as gone before. It was certainly followed by a spate of parodies.

A Lost Chord Found

We stood alone in the choir loft
  By the organ tall and grim,
While over the keys her fingers
  Followed their own sweet whim;
I spoke of the coming parting,
  And plead for one farewell kiss,
But her modest wish forbade me
  Lest the sexton old might list.
Then I struck on the organ a strong, full chord,
  And ere its echoes died,
In the twilight dim of the old gray church
  I kissed my promised bride.

We stood again by the organ
  When many years had fled,
But she thought me grown cold and heartless,
  And I thought her old love dead.
I spoke of our last fond parting,
  Of the chord and its tender tide,
And how like the sound of that music
  Our love had throbbed and died –
Then my heart leaped up with a great glad bound
  And forgot its recent pain,
For she blushed and, dropping her lashes, said,
  'Could you find me that chord again?'

Willard Holcomb

Samuel Taylor Coleridge and his loud bassoon

Coleridge's famous line from *The Ancient Mariner*,

> The Wedding-Guest here beat his breast
> For he heard the loud bassoon . . .

shows that he misunderstood the sort of noise a bassoon would have made in 1798, when he wrote the poem. As we now know thanks to the 'authentic' movement and hundreds of replica and original instruments, eighteenth-century bassoons were played with a softer, broader reed than the modern instrument, which makes a much cruder, firmer sound. What Coleridge should have written was:

> The Wedding-Guest here beat his breast
> For he heard the gentle, buzzing-like-a-bumble-bee-
> trapped-in-a-jam-jar bassoon . . .

But it would have ruined his scansion. At least he did not call it 'The Joker of the Orchestra', as so many more recent authors have done. I have yet to find out who coined the phrase: probably some writer of *Analytical Notes* paid by the line. In truth, for every comic passage like the rollicking tune in *The Sorcerer's Apprentice* by Dukas, there are hundreds of lyrical or sad ones. Far from being the orchestral comedian the bassoon is the orchestral answer to the tearful, sobbing tenor; and the alto register of the instrument can sound even more pathetic, in the best sense of the word. Mozart was well aware of this, for in many of his works for wind instruments, especially the glorious serenades, the bassoon always gets passages, or even whole variations, in the minor key. This is a well-defined Mozart fingerprint.

A Yorkshire *Messiah*

The name of one Victorian hopeful has unfortunately not come down to us but it belonged to a Yorkshire composer who in 1895 offered the publishers Novello & Co a brand new *Messiah* he had composed – to the same words as Handel's, which after all were long out of copyright (if they were ever in). He added that he felt sure 'the public would now like a change from Handel's music to my own'. When the publishers made his offer public they felt moved to protect the confident composer from ridicule by withholding his name, which is a pity; but it was rumoured that Novellos cherished the manuscript and kept it under lock and key.

This courageous Yorkshireman was not the first to follow Handel. The German composer A J Romberg (1767-1821) similarly had no inhibitions about setting the twice-sacred text, an oratorio called, like Handel's German version, *Der Messias*, to words adapted by Friedrich Gottlieb Klopstock (1724-1803), and from the same sources as Jennens trawled for the Handel oratorio.

It is thought that Beethoven also had plans to write a *Messiah*, which would probably have opened up the field to all comers. And incidentally, those who self-righteously maintain that it is a blunder to say *The Messiah* with the definite article, claiming that it should be just *Messiah*, are wrong: it is an untenable theory proposed by Julian Herbage in the 1950s. Handel referred to it both as 'my *Messiah*' and 'my oratorio *The Messiah*' which, as it is *Der Messias* in German, would have come naturally to him. Perhaps Charles E Horn, a prolific composer of popular and tuneful songs, found a more original oratorio subject: at Easter 1845 the Melophonic Society gave the first performance of his oratorio *Satan*.

An Irish *Messiah*

An Irish *Messiah* performance by the Portadown Philharmonic Society in 1898 was comprehensively criticized in the *Ulster Times*. Its music critic was not a man easily pleased – yet his notice was refreshingly free from the critical jargon of the time. To savour it best these extracts should be read aloud in a strong brogue after the consumption of half-a-dozen pints of draught Guinness:

> The delivery and reading of some of the choruses was absurd. The Hallélujah Chorus, for example, was turned out worse than any other chorus in the book – that is, having regard to its capabilities. It was stiff, monotonous and heavy. It was one long, dull moan of dread indifference … As artists they could not sit down properly, and rising, they came down in batches at a time … Their pronunciation was horrid, and bad beyond anything we had ever heard before … the sopranos were simply execrable. They screamed their Fs until their voices cracked and tore into shreds. The Hallelujah Chorus was simply butchered, and the life thrashed out of it … The tenor took 'Every Valley' as if after a good dinner and he was about to lounge in peace and contentment with the world. His stage manner wants patching. The soprano was either looking over her shoulder at the conductor, or up through her front hair at him … She carried her score over her left arm much as a hotel waiter carries his napkin or duster … As soon as she has finished her solo she ignores the existence of the instruments, and gives a tug at the end of it, then throws the symphony at us much in the same way as one throws a bone at a dog, and with a snap of her jaw and a glance of her grand eyes says: 'There now, you've got it. Much good may it do you!' In the air 'But who may abide' the bass was simply, to use a vulgar expression, out of it. In fact Mr Kelly was afraid to open his mouth, the contour of which is rather flat, and not such a mouth as could give proper expression to an awful warning like this.

And a Lancashire Gilbert and Sullivan

Not only was there a Yorkshire and an Irish *Messiah*, a Lancashire Gilbert and Sullivan might also have emerged, depending on the response to the following advertisement in *The Musical Times* of October 1891:

> A Gilbertian librettist and Sullivanesque melodist wishes correspondence with first-class orchestral arranger. Gentleman of means indispensable. With a View to Collaboration and production of Comic Opera. Advertiser is a popular song writer. Address Savoy, 23 St Peter's Square, Preston, Lancashire.

But no takers for Stainer

First singer: What do you think about Stainer's *Crucifixion?*
Second Singer: Bloody good idea.

The village choir

Half a bar, half a bar
Half a bar onward!
Into an awful ditch
Choir and conductor hitch
Into a mess of pitch
Led the Old Hundred.

Trebles to right of them,
Tenors to left of them,

Basses in front of them,
Bellowed and thundered.

Oh that conductor's look
When the sopranos took
Each their own time and hook
From the Old Hundred.

Screeched all the trebles here,
Boggled the tenors there,
Raising the parson's hair
While his mind wandered.

Theirs not to reason why
This Psalm was pitched too high,
Theirs but to gasp and cry
Out the Old Hundred.

Trebles to right of them,
Tenors to left of them,
Basses in front of them
Bellowed and thundered.

Stormed they with shout and yell
Not wise they sang nor well,
Drowning the sexton's bell,
While the church wondered.

Dire the conductor's glare
Flashed his pitchfork in air
Sounding fresh keys to bear
Out the Old Hundred.

Swiftly he turned his back,
Reached he his hat from rack,
Then from the screaming pack
Himself he sundered.

Tenors to right of him,

Tenors to left of him,
Discords behind him
Bellowed and thundered.

Oh the wild howls they wrought,
Right to the end they fought,
Some tune they sang but not,
Not the Old Hundred.

Anonymous

New Parson (having noticed that the double-bass player uses his left hand simply to support the instrument): I SEE YOU DON'T USE YOUR FINGERS WHEN YOU PLAY, JOHN.
John: NOA, SIR; YE SEE THERE BE SOME AS TWIDDLES THEIR FINGERS WHEN THEY PLAY, AN' THERE BE SOME AS DON'T, AN' I BE ONE O' THEY THAT DON'T.

(By kind permission of *Punch*)
1911

7

Music expresses nothing
Igor Stravinsky

Music expresses nothing

That is what Igor Stravinsky said – not in the interrogative but as an *ex cathedra* pronouncement: 'Music expresses nothing.' His sweeping statement used to be much quoted, and as he said it when he was widely regarded as the greatest living composer nobody apparently questioned it. It is much less often heard today, for it probably tells one more about Stravinsky and his machine rhythms than it does about music. Next to smells, music is the most powerful stimulus for stirring memories, for conjuring up certain associations, for putting people in one mood or another: love, when it is soft and gentle, or war, when the trumpets start to bray and drums beat out a martial rhythm. 'They're playing our tune' may be using a boring old cliché, but it has much truth in it.

Radio producers are only too well aware of this and have at their disposal a vast stock of clichés designed to set the scene and evoke the atmosphere of a programme. Whenever some news, feature or holiday programme sets out to describe a certain country, a standard-issue burst of music is available.

Ever since the *Maigret* television series, a French atmosphere is invariably conjured up by a few seconds of wheezing accordions.

A Greek holiday scene? Bring out the old *Never on Sunday* bazouki.

Austria or Bavaria? Reach for a tape of thigh-slapping oom-pah music.

Spain – the clacking castanets and twanging guitars will be brought out.

Hawaiian guitars take us straight to the Pacific islands.

Japan and China to share the same clanging gongs; gamelans for Malaysia.

Cowbells spell Switzerland but there is no suitable music, it seems, for Belgium or Luxembourg.

Whenever a report about athletics is in the offing someone is sure to start beating those tin cans that introduced the feeble little up-and-down Vangelis tune we know from *Chariots of Fire*.

So, Mr Stravinsky, music expresses a great deal.

For at least five centuries Programme Music has been trying to tell stories and paint pictures but not always succeeding. It is easy to put this to the test. Perhaps the most familiar examples of eighteenth-century programme music are the *Four Seasons* of Vivaldi. But which is which? No one can tell, without having it spelt out beforehand, whether at any given moment he is listening to Spring, Summer, Autumn or Winter.

The Victorian composer Francesco Berger once composed a piece for piano and, while he was composing it, imagined a strict sequence of events, giving a bar-by-bar account of certain images that went through his mind – in other words, a 'programme'; but he kept it to himself. Then he played the piece to three of his fellow composers and asked each to write down what he thought the music portrayed. The first, who happened to be a Welshman, said, in perfect seriousness, that the piece to him, meant 'Daybreak as seen from the lowest gallery of a Welsh coal-mine.' The second declared it was 'A boar hunt in Russia'; and the third musician said *he* thought the piano piece suggested 'An enamoured couple whispering love vows.' Only then did the composer reveal what *he* had tried to illustrate: 'The discovery by Pharaoh's daughter of the infant Moses in the bulrushes.'

When a lady complimented Richard Strauss on the realism of his tone poem *Don Juan* and claimed to have been able to picture to herself a succession of the hero's conquests, the composer replied, 'Yes, and did you notice one of the girls had red hair?' On the other hand Strauss himself wrote down a list of events depicting the action of *Till Eulenspiegel*; and related them to certain bar numbers. He also revealed that those rather rude whooping noises by the horns heard at the beginning of his opera *Der Rosenkavalier* portray in music what takes place on the sofa, just before the curtain rises, between the countess and her young lover Oktavian.

When Sir John Barbirolli rehearsed the Prelude to Wagner's *Tristan and Isolde* he sometimes pointed with a wink and a nudge at the exact bar in the *Vorspiel* where the foreplay becomes consummation. In another of his tone poems, *Don Quixote*, Strauss himself gives a graphic description of the scene where the hero is frightened by a flock of sheep. But had he attempted to do so without mimicking the bleating of sheep no one would have been any the wiser. Later, when he wrote *Bourgeois Gentilhomme*, he quotes in the supper scene the very same passage of the sheep, as a kind of musical pun to let hearers know that the diners were now eating mutton.

Going back to the seventeenth century, one finds the German composer Johann Kuhnau (J S Bach's immediate predecessor at St Thomas's Church in Leipzig) writing a series of harpsichord works purporting to describe scenes from the Bible. The pieces were issued in 1700 as 'Biblical Sonatas', giving, among other scenes, a blow-by-blow description of the fight between David and Goliath. And again the composer has to help listeners out by supplying them with a programme of what happens. From this we see that it takes just one bar of C major scales for the pebble to travel from David's catapult to Goliath's forehead.

Handel, in his oratorio *Israel in Egypt*, makes equally formalized attempts to illustrate flies, hailstones and frogs – and whenever the latter appear in a piece of music you may be sure the notes hop about in wide leaps – as surely as every mention of frogs in English tabloid newspapers is certain to describe someone as 'hopping mad'. In Handel's *Orlando* the music goes into five-four time, then just about the maddest time signature imaginable, to show that his subject had been struck by madness. What would he have made of Stravinsky's time changes?

Ever since the middle of the eighteenth century, composers have been writing musical pieces depicting sleigh rides. Leopold Mozart (father of Wolfgang Amadeus) wrote his Sleigh ride, or *Schlittenfahrt* (you can guess what English orchestral players call them), in 1755, Wolfgang his Sleigh ride, still with the same recognizable clichés, almost 40 years later. Sleighs were like horse-drawn coaches, driven by coachmen or postilions, but because these vehicles glided along silently in the snow, without any clatter of wheels, the horses that drew them had sleigh bells fixed to them, to warn pedestrians of their approach: a gift to any composer. All he needed was some sleigh bells, a jig-jogging tempo and winter was here. This convention has continued down the centuries, all the way to Delius's as well as Leroy Anderson's sleigh rides.

Horses are more problematical, in spite of the fact that the trumpet can produce a startlingly convincing neigh, and every percussion box contains a selection of clip-clopping coconut shells. Yet when Schubert wrote his *Erlkönig*, he no more than hinted at the clattering of hooves, simply but graphically, in the piano accompaniment. The words of the song make it clear what he is on about. But after his death his brother Ferdinand made an orchestral arrangement of the Erl King, spelling things out without a vocal part, in which the Narrator was played by a Flute, the Child by a Clarinet, the Father by a Bass Trombone, and the Erl King himself by a Horn in B flat; unfortunately the arrangement has been lost, so there is no way of telling who played the Horse.

Another favourite and highly formalized kind of programme music was the Battle Symphony, popular during the eighteenth and nineteenth centuries – the biggest and most famous example being that by Beethoven. Such symphonies were as formally drawn up and stylized as the real battle lines of their day, often employing two orchestras placed on either side of a stage, one side almost literally firing notes against the other – stereophonic performances of their time. And of course here, too, ancient clichés are adhered to and which even the conventions-shunning Beethoven observed: rattling side drums for small-arms fire, timpani and bass drums for the heavier artillery and whining violins for 'the cries of the wounded'.

Composers, egged on by publishers, were ready at the drop of a field-marshal's hat to produce a Battle Symphony about whatever battle happened to be in the news – and on at least one occasion came badly unstuck. In the 1860s, when the British Empire experienced some little local difficulty in Africa and found that the Emperor of Abyssinia was being tiresome, things came to a head when he had the temerity to intercept diplomatic mail and imprison the British consul, who had quite properly protested about the Emperor's cruelties to his own people. In those days the British stood no nonsense from foreigners, so in the Queen's Speech of 1867 Parliament declared war on the Abyssinian Emperor and sent an expeditionary force to Africa to sort him out. At home, John Pridham, a popular composer in his day, was ready at his post and composed a descriptive battle piece for piano, entitled 'The Battle of Abyssinia'. It portrayed in music the sounds of the cavalry charge, the rattling of the guns and the cries of the wounded; and the piece ended with the customary, final, triumphant rendering of 'God Save the Queen'.

Music engraving was slow, the expeditionary force took some time to steam to Africa, and news of its progress travelled back equally slowly. Pridham's publishers wanted his music in the shops as soon as the expected news of the inevitable victory had reached these shores. Unfortunately, things didn't quite work out as he thought. The natives surrendered without so much as a shot being fired, King Theodore committed suicide, and there was no battle. Nevertheless, English music shops were flooded with copies of the 'Battle of Abyssinia' that never was. The nation's piano stools and later the second-hand shops still occasionally turn up copies. If there was ever a battle in or near Prague it bore no resemblance to the 'descriptive piece' entitled 'The Battle of Prague', a purely imaginary event portrayed by the notorious forger Franz Kotzwara. It is the one original work he is remembered for.

Even the sinking of the *Titanic* in 1912 produced a crop of unbelievably tasteless 'descriptive' musical piano pieces. Their immediate publication was sheer sensationalism, the final throes of the musical penny broadside. One of these *Titanic* pieces has a descending scale passage, with the printed explanation – 'Lowering the lifeboats'; and the piece ends, rather tactlessly, with 'A life on the ocean wave'. Within days of the disaster songs were issued on cylinder recordings: 'Stand to your post' and 'Be British!', both versifying some of the alleged calls by the captain and crew of the *Titanic* and the band's alleged performance of 'Nearer my God to Thee' to calm the passengers' nerves (a cruel fiction, for had they played it they would have reminded them that death was near).

But the most far-fetched pieces of programme music have always been cheap imports from abroad. After an attempt on the life of Bismarck, the German composer Julius Grauer wrote an epic *Sinfonia attentatica*, or 'Assassination Symphony', complete with the near-fatal pistol shot (a sound traditionally made by giving the rim of the side drum a smart blow with a stick). The assassin missed.

The Anglo-French composer Sir George Onslow (1784-1853), who in spite of his English name and baronet's title, was a member of the French aristocracy, was fond of hunting (which in France means with a rifle, not horses and hounds). In his mid-forties and out with the hunt, he accidentally shot himself in the face, injuring his ear and damaging his hearing. His next work, a string quintet, was called The Bullet Quintet, which contains movements entitled Fever and Delirium, Convalescence and Cure.

Half a century later, Smetana, in his autobiographical string quartet 'From my Life', also illustrated his own ear affliction, a tinnitus (ringing in the ears), which in his case was on a top E, dramatically introduced into the quartet, played on the violin. Not long afterwards the tinnitus sent him into a lunatic asylum, where he died insane.

From the other side of the Atlantic came news in 1932 that two musically inclined medical doctors had demonstrated their dual talents. A Canadian physician, Dr Forde McLoughlin of Toronto, entertained the assembled members of the Canadian Medical Association with a performance of a new grand work composed for the occasion. It was scored for full orchestra and entitled 'Influenza – a Tone Poem'. Then, in 1948, a Dr Herman M Parris of Philadelphia presented to the Doctors' Orchestral Society of New York a ten-movement orchestral suite entitled 'The Hospital', which describes in music a young woman's operation for removal of the appendix. The suite includes movements entitled 'The Operating Room' (Allegro, leading to Molto agitato); 'A Pre-Operation Prayer' (Andantino); 'A Nurse' (Allegro amabile) and 'Anaesthesia' (Presto).

But even that startling piece of musico-medical programme music was not a new idea. The seventeenth-century French viola-da-gamba player and composer Marin Marais wrote a musical description of an operation for the removal of a stone. The sections are headed, 'The Aspect of the Operating Table', 'The Instruments', 'The Patient Mounts the Table', 'He Is Apprehensive and Tries to Flee', 'His Limbs Are Bound with Silken Cords', 'The Incision', 'The Blood Flows' and, finally, 'The Forceps Are Inserted and the Stone Is Removed', 'The Patient is Put in Bed to Recover'. The sonata is concluded by a 'General Dance of Rejoicing' – presumably for the surgeon and nurses, without the participation of the patient.

Wife: FRED! DO YOU MIND STOPPING FOR A MINUTE? I WANT TO ASK MRS TIDSWELL IF SHE CAN SPARE ME SOME COTTON WOOL FOR MY EARS.

(By kind permission of *Punch*)

1933

Lights out – Manchester *c* 1986

The BBC Philharmonic Orchestra was recording a new work by a young contemporary composer (who shall be nameless here because by the early 1990s he was beginning to make a name for himself) when the lights failed and Studio 7 was plunged into total darkness. The work was what orchestral players call 'squeaky door-hinge' music: even when they follow the written notes in front of them, this kind of music sounds to them, and to most listeners, random and senseless. Thus, when the lights went out they just continued playing – anything that came into their heads or fell under their fingers. I have a tape of the recording which I use as a party quiz game. Can anyone 'spot the join' and say where the composer's laboriously written work stopped and the musicians' off-the-cuff improvisation begins?

Lights out – Vienna *c* 1970

At a concert given by the Vienna Philharmonic the lights went out during the final pages of the final work in the concert, Beethoven's 'Eroica'. Once again the hall was in darkness, and the musicians could see neither their notes nor the conductor, Karl Böhm. Nevertheless they continued playing, from memory. Just before the coda, where the music slows down and becomes softer, a player at the back called out in a loud voice (and in a broad Viennese accent difficult to anglicize), 'Is 'e still there? Or has 'e gone home?'

Lights out – Vilnius 1900

The Violin Times of 15 April 1900 rather pointlessly reported a light failure in the capital city of Lithuania, telling us little more than that solo violin recitalists, then as now, played from memory:

> M Ondricek displayed a wonderful presence of mind during a concert at Wilna. Whilst playing the G minor Fugue of Bach the electric light suddenly went out, and the concert room, which was crowded, was left in utter darkness. M Ondricek, however, went on playing quietly as if nothing had happened, thus preventing a panic among the audience. When the hall was again lit up, the artist received tremendous ovations and thanks for his presence of mind.

Knowing it backwards?

During the 1980s BBC Radio 3 broadcast the first performance of a new composition by a young woman composer, the kind who compose not in a study or sitting room but in a 'sound laboratory'. Whether by accident or wicked design, the sound engineer wound the tape on to its spool the wrong way round, so that the performance came out back-to-front. The only person to telephone the BBC was the composer herself. No one else – listeners, producer and sound engineer – realized that anything was amiss, and even the composer's complaint took some time to reach its destination. After an apology the tape was rewound and played again in the right direction, but listeners could still not tell any difference.

Playing music *al rovescio* (or backwards) is, of course an old contrapuntal trick, much practised by eighteenth-century composers, especially when writing canons. But the agreed requirement of such a palindrome was that it should sound like a convincing piece of music both ways. Anyone can simply write out a piece backwards. A piece which sounds random when played one way is likely to sound just as random when played back-to-front.

A Scottish record company which, under the Waverley label, specialized in bagpipe music, issued a disc during the 1960s featuring performances by a well-known pipe band. Again, when the discs were pressed, the master tape of the entire record had been processed from a tape that was accidentally played back-to-front. Many copies were sold before the error was spotted, for bagpipe music, which has no telltale gaps or pauses, lends itself to such treatment. To the untrained ear it might even sound pleasant both ways.

One of the most enterprising smaller English companies, Saydisc (which has an unrivalled list of ethnic, archival and mechanical music) suffered a misfortune unique in the annals of music. An LP entitled *Kitten on the Keys – Popular Music from Pianola Rolls* (SDL 355) issued in 1986 – contains a splendid and unique collection of performances by mechanical pianos from the Roy Mickleburgh Collection. This time someone made a small error when inserting the piano roll of the title number into its slot on the pianola in such a way that the perforated paper roll of Zez Confrey's all-time hit was slotted in laterally inverted. The result is a kind of mirror canon *al rovescio* which not even Johann Sebastian Bach achieved, for *Kitten on the Keys* is played in such a way that the high notes become low notes and passages that go up in the original, go down. Amazingly it is still instantly recognizable as *Kitten on the Keys*.

According to an old joke (which can be told about almost any celebrated composition teacher) a pupil of Serge Prokofiev confessed that he found composition difficult. The teacher said, 'I'll let you into a secret. All you have to do is take an existing composition, turn it upside-down and copy it out, adding a few wrong notes.' The pupil went home and, in homage to his master, took one of his early works, put it on the piano upside-down – and there was Beethoven's Moonlight Sonata.

Jacques Thibaut is uncoupled

Much as the violinist Jacques Thibaut (1880-1953) loved music he loved women more. On one of his concert tours in Russia he met a beautiful girl on the Trans-Siberian Express. As the train passed Omsk they lunched together in the dining-car, at Tomsk (or wherever) they had dinner, and then, having reached an understanding, somewhere on the way to Nijzni Novgorod he joined her in her sleeping cabin. Next morning, as he prepared to make his way back to his own compartment he found that that part of the train had been uncoupled at Sibirinovostni and he was stranded in Siberia in his dressing-gown, without clothes, documents or violin.

She (having played a little thing for Bertram): I HOPE YOU DIDN'T HEAR THE WRONG NOTE!
Bertram (thinking to be complimentary): WHICH ONE?

(By kind permission of *Punch*)
1901

Composers love birdsong

Birdsong combines uncommonly well with instrumental music, and numerous composers have found inspiration in it. The two notes of the cuckoo have appeared in compositions since the Middle Ages: one of Handel's Organ Concertos as well as a song by Mahler are both based on a contest between a cuckoo and a nightingale; and during the eighteenth century two-note cuckoo whistles were often called for in the so-called Toy Symphonies to charming effect, together with imitation-nightingale bird warblers (traditionally filled with gin or some other colourless spirit), quail noises and rattles.

Numerous birdcalls have appeared in symphonies, most notably in the slow movement of Beethoven's Pastoral Symphony. Open-air performances are invariably enhanced by comments from feathered members of the audience; but Ottorino Respighi (1879-1936) in his symphonic poem *The Pines of Rome*, describing four pine groves in and around Rome, used what in 1923-4 was the newest technology: a gramophone hidden in the middle of the orchestra which at a predestined point played a record of a nightingale. Before tape recorders made this effect more practical, the task of gently lowering the tone-arm on to a scratchy 78 rpm disc used to fall to someone sitting among the upper woodwind players. When the record was put on clumsily, and a heavy, old-fashioned gramophone tone-arm skidded across the disc, the atmosphere could be effectively ruined.

During a performance in Paris of Schubert's 'Unfinished' Symphony given by the Berlin Philharmonic Orchestra under the Austrian conductor Artur Nikisch (1855-1922), 'a flock of sparrows settled on a window-sill and joined in', according to Debussy, who was present in his capacity of music critic and described the occasion; he added that 'Nikisch had the grace not to demand their expulsion'. This is in contrast with an extraordinarily unfeeling blunder committed by someone during a recital in 1979 by the Austrian guitarist Konrad Ragnossnig. The concert was held in an English country church and was being recorded by the BBC, when a solitary sparrow perched on a beam and decided to trill an obbligato to the guitar. According to the tabloid press, which made much of the incident (and probably embellished it) the vicar said, 'It was absolutely impossible. The artist just could not start. He is a true professional, and you know what these chaps are like ...' Wrong: a true professional should be able to keep his concentration in the face of a few gentle extraneous twittering noises. Nevertheless, reported the papers, 'the vicar's son was called, and with his air rifle summarily executed the sparrow'. It was not only a musical blunder but also a religious one, as the Bible in several passages expressly praises the sparrows' appearance in church together with human voices, and exhorts man to tolerate them. Mozart's Mass, K220, is nicknamed the 'Sparrow Mass' (*Spatzenmesse*), supposedly because of some pecking, staccato fiddle figures. But such violinistic devices appear in countless eighteenth-century orchestral works, and I suspect that the name is more likely be a reference to choirboys, nicknamed *Spatzen* in German.

In England, the choral scholars at Eton College were always nicknamed 'canaries' and these, too, are affectionately described in many musical works: most popularly in a florid and difficult nineteenth-century violin solo, as well as in a contredanse by Mozart and an entire cantata by Telemann, in which a sweetly singing canary is eaten by a blunderous cat.

The musical no-shows

The performer who cancels, or worse, simply fails to show up, is the bane of concert promoters, alienates audiences and sends concert agents to an early grave. A famous guitarist, much in demand and a great player, habitually kept his audiences guessing: would he or would he not appear? He usually wouldn't. During the 1980s one of the superstars of the *Nessun dorma* circuit produced medical evidence that he suffered from Stage Dust Allergy and would be unable to appear as contracted. It was a new kind of allergy – even to doctors among the potential audience, who had all paid good money to book their tickets; but nobody, not even a doctor, can dispute a doctor's note.

Disappointed customers, having queued for their seats in the first place, gritted their teeth and patiently stood in line for a second time to get their money back. They were even more furious when they saw in the evening papers that the singer had been discovered sunning himself on a tropical island in the company of a young woman instead of braving the dank weather in the metropolis. Fortunately this rest cure miraculously cleared up his Stage Dust Allergy and no further attacks were reported.

The great Polish piano virtuoso Ignaz Paderewski (1860-1941) was the most adored, over-hyped and over-rated of all pianists. Percy Scholes wrote, 'The general public lacked discrimination and worshipped him on all occasions alike – even when he crashed out hard tone, phrased illogically and pedalled badly. His general popularity was, from first to last, quite unrivalled by any contemporary.' For his recitals, 'those not provided with reserved seats began to arrive seven hours in advance'. It was obviously not all puff, publicity and clever public relations, but his surviving piano rolls and gramophone recordings reveal nothing out of the ordinary. By today's standards he might have found it difficult to be shortlisted in the Warsaw Piano Competition, let alone made it as a finalist in Moscow. George Bernard Shaw described him as 'a man of various moods ... alert, humorous, delightful ... sensational, empty, vulgar and violent ... dignified, almost sympathetic' (he was also grossly overworked, and must have been one of the first musicians to describe symptoms of what would now be called Repetitive Strain Injury).

But above all, Paderewski was a capricious canceller of

engagements. In 1895 it was the turn of the music lovers of Torquay to be disappointed, at short notice, having braved foul weather to hear him. They took their revenge in an anonymous verse, the kind of gentle but wickedly barbed satire the British excel in:

The Talk of Torquay

Said the people of Torquay,
'Oh, my goodness, do you see?
Paderewski's shortly coming down from town,
With his pianistic feats
And the prices of the seats
Seems, just like the great performer, coming down?'

Said the people of Torquay,
'We're all going, there will be
An enormous crowd of people in the hall;
And before he goes away
He will make a good day's pay,
Though he charges but five shillings for a stall.'

Said the mighty Mr P,
'Do you dare suggest to me
I should play to wretched beggars such as these?
You will want me after that,
Me, to carry round the hat,
And to let the people give me what they please!'

Said the people of Torquay,
'Disregarding snowstorms we
Struggled here through weather execrably bleak.
What is this? He will not play?
He has calmly gone away?
We should say of lesser men, Well that is cheek!'

Said the people of Torquay,
'We might almost think that he
Was an autocratic emperor, a tsar;
    Only kings are more polite,
    There is no one who is quite
So conceited as these foreign players are.'

And the thought occurs to me,
'*One* five shillings, that would be
More than poor Beethoven had per day.
    But Beethoven, who was he
    When compared to Mr P,
Or to any of the gentlemen who play?'

Another celebrated artist notorious for his unreliability was the tenor John Sims Reeves (1818-1900), and the cumulative evidence of cancellation announcements printed in many successive decades of *The Musical Times* suggests that more column-inches were devoted to his cancellations than his performances: 'Has any singer of our country pleased and disappointed more audiences than Sims Reeves – pleased them every time they heard him sing and disappointed them every time they heard, instead, that "owing to indisposition Mr Sims Reeves will not be able to appear"?' It seems he started to be 'indisposed' some time before 1859 (though a brief report in an earlier issue of *The Musical Times* has an organist 'Mr Reeves' failing to appear – and the young Sims was indeed an organist before he became a singer).

In the 1859 Gloucester Festival Reeves appeared in the first part of the programme but failed to return for the second. The long account in *The Musical Times* tells how one of the stewards made an announcement that '... roused applause and hisses: As Mr Sims Reeves has quietly walked off, the stewards cannot fetch him back and I hope they will not be blamed.' The mayor of Gloucester then walked on and made a similar 'what can we do?' announcement, which was 'answered with shouts of laughter'.

After that one disappointment followed another. *The Musical Times* in 1866 reports 'the absence of Mr Sims Reeves from indisposition', two months later, 'the severe indisposition of the gentleman ...' and in December, 'Mr Reeves, for whom an apology was made on the score of indisposition'. At the Welsh Eisteddfodd there were 'hisses and groans' and 'disrespectful comments' (I can just hear them, for the Welsh take their Eisteddfodau very seriously). In Greenock the singer caused 'a minor riot' because he refused to sing until a baby that 'uttered a piercing shriek' was removed (good for him!) and in Oxford he got the blame for an unconscionable delay in appearing on the platform ('the blame being expressed in a very forcible manner indeed'). For once he was blamed unfairly, as his accompanist had suffered a fainting fit, but his reputation had preceded him. He was, however, meticulous about returning his fee – usually a hundred guineas, an immense sum in those days.

Inevitably, in the end Reeves was sued for failing to honour a contract. It came as no surprise to read that the magistrate, like so many of his audiences, waited in vain: Sims failed to appear in court and was fined ten pounds in his absence, in spite of a:

Certificate from an accredited member of the medical profession, which was produced in court, Mr Reeves was suffering from a severe cold and sore throat so that it would have been extremely dangerous for him to leave the house. In spite of this official assurance it was decided that he ought to have sung, and he was cast in damages to the amount of £23, and £10 fine ...

He appealed, and the appeal was upheld; but as 'Mr Reeves was compelled to travel down to Cheltenham when he should have been singing [in London] at Mr Leslie's concert ...' he again evoked the customary groans and hisses, this time from the disappointed Mr Leslie and his audience.

Sims Reeves spent the last eleven years of his life giving farewell recitals, but took the precaution of having Mr W H Cummings standing by to sing his farewells for him when he was 'unfortunately indisposed and unable to appear'. Sims was clearly a troubled performer, though there was never any suggestion of chronic ill health. Perhaps he did have a chronic throat condition, which would not have stopped him from appearing as an organist or, more likely, some recurring crisis of confidence, to which even the most consummate artists are subject.

In his last years the great Viennese conductor and Mahler interpreter Jascha Horenstein was several times obliged to cancel through his increasing frailty, and his planned final visit to Manchester, to conduct the BBC Northern Orchestra, had to be called off. It was to have been a recording in the Milton Hall, not a big enough studio to permit the presence of an audience but there was room for interested members of the public, provided they did not applaud or bring babies emitting piercing shrieks. Horenstein's place was taken at short notice by the Scottish conductor Bryden (Jack) Thomson, who regularly worked with the BBCNO. A little later, after a subsequent date with the orchestra as an extra player, I had a drink in the pub conveniently housed in the same building, and was accosted by another customer, who had been present at the concert. 'This fellow 'orensteen,' he said. 'Went to his recording the other day and afterwards he was in 'ere having a drink. Got talking to him. He's a fraud, you know. Bloody Scotsman, he is.'

Keep your eye on the fellow to your left

Until comparatively recently the deputy system used to be rife in London, a system that permitted one player to subcontract another to take his place, at either rehearsal or performance. Conductors hated it, because they could never be certain that a musician who attended rehearsal, and who had enjoyed the benefit of his instructions, would be present to carry them out on the night.

It was Sir Henry Wood who finally reduced its worst excesses, and it led directly to the founding of the London Symphony Orchestra – formed by a breakaway group of players who refused Wood's guaranteed offer of annual engagements worth £100, on condition that they never sent a deputy. Standards of orchestral playing have now increased to a point where few players would risk their jobs by sending along even the finest deputy. At the same time, deputizing is fraught with danger for players, too, as they have to strike a balance between finding someone competent enough not to let them down, but not so good as to show them up; in which case the deputy might in the long term deprive them of the job. Ben Trovato tells a story about a trombonist who was

THE EXTREME PENALTY
She: WHAT DO YOU THINK OF HIS EXECUTION?
He: I'M IN FAVOUR OF IT.

(By kind permission of *Punch*)
1907

offered a more lucrative engagement than the theatre job he filled every night, but could not find a deputy. In desperation he took his spare trombone to the pub next to the theatre and offered a customer the chance of earning a few bob. 'All you have to do is put it to your mouth and pretend to blow. Just squint to the left and keep your eye on the fellow to your left: just do what he does.' When the overture started he did just that – and found the fellow on his left anxiously squinting to the right.

Beware the font

Ovide Musin, the violinist, was the victim of an odd accident recently. His concert company was about to begin an evening entertainment at a Baptist church, and Mr Musin, arrayed in faultless evening dress, thought he would view the audience without being seen. To accomplish this purpose he stepped behind a curtain which hung at the back of the platform. There was a splash, and the violinist found himself in three feet of water. He emerged a very wet and angry man. Mr Musin had inadvertently stepped into the baptismal font. It was after eight o'clock, and the concert had begun. A young man came to the violinist's rescue, however, and said he would provide Mr Musin with a dry outfit. But it was half an hour before he did, and Mr Musin was several minutes late in making his appearance. The new trousers fitted him rather awkwardly, and he was not in a pleasant frame of mind, but he got through with his part of the programme, and the audience is probably still ignorant of the fact that he had fallen into the font.

Musical News, June 1893

A cautionary tale

My colleague Robert Braga, former principal viola of the Royal Liverpool Philharmonic, told me a cautionary tale about the wisdom of string players always carrying spare strings. He and three colleagues, all four of them fresh from college, were about to give a concert in a rural music club. They walked on, were greeted with polite applause, sat down and were about to start the first quartet, bows poised, when snap, the leader's A string broke. He apologized and left the platform to fit another string. To his dismay he found he had no spare in his fiddle case. From the wings he beckoned to his second, who walked off to join him. He had no spare A string either. Then the viola player, wondering what the delay was, also walked off, leaving the cellist all alone on the platform.

All this was observed by the audience with good-natured, sporting amusement: English spectators love small emergencies, which loosen the tension and stimulate much more applause after the performance. But there was no performance. The three players offstage made signs to the cellist, who joined them for a hurried conference, and after trying in vain to knot the two ends of the string together they decided the only thing they could do was pack their instruments and quietly steal away. Music and music stands, which they could ill afford to lose, were sacrificed.

Sherlock Holmes mistreats his mahogany violin

Whenever a Sherlock Holmes play, film or television series is produced about Sir Arthur Conan Doyle's gentleman detective and his side-kick Dr Watson, a violin is sure to lend background colour, either played offstage while the actor inadequately 'mimes' the action (it never looks convincing unless he actually knows a little of how to play) or, in broadcasts, accompanied by a tape recording. For according to Doyle, playing the violin was Holmes's favourite relaxation after a hard day's peering through his magnifying glass. But what was his playing like? After all, his creator cast him in the image of the true renaissance man, learned in many and various disciplines.

In *A Study in Scarlet*, Dr Watson describes Holmes's fiddle technique, at the same time giving a hint as to his musical taste:

> His powers upon the violin ... were remarkable, but as eccentric as all his other accomplishments. That he could play pieces, and difficult pieces, I knew well, because at my request he has played me some of Mendelssohn's *Lieder*, and other favourites.

Most remarkable, my dear Watson. It is unlikely that Holmes would have found the vocal line of Mendelssohn songs, unaccompanied by a piano, musically satisfactory. Doyle probably meant Mendelssohn's *Lieder ohne Worte*, the famous 'Songs without Words', which were written for piano alone. It seems unlikely that Holmes would have 'scraped away' at the right-hand part of the piano version. His playing posture, too, was highly original:

> Leaning back in his armchair of an evening, he would close his eyes and scrape carelessly at the fiddle which was thrown across his knee. Sometimes the chords were sonorous and melancholy, sometimes fantastic and cheerful ... and reflected the thoughts which possessed him, but whether the music aided those thoughts, or whether the playing was simply the result of a whim or fancy, was more than I could determine. I might have rebelled against these exasperating solos had it not been that he usually terminated them by playing in quick succession a selection of my favourite airs as a slight compensation for the trial upon my patience.

Guy Warrack, in his *Sherlock Holmes and Music*, fancifully suggests that these 'chords' represented an attempt by Holmes to play Bach's great unaccompanied Chaconne in D minor; but I doubt it. Unless he was a contortionist with a triple-jointed left forearm it would have been impossible for him to play the double- or triple-stopping which that great work demands, while he had his violin so carelessly 'thrown across his knee'.

So, far from attempting Bach's difficult Chaconne, Holmes probably played some of Watson's 'favourite airs'; and whatever these were they would not have been musically demanding, either for him or Holmes. There is no indication that Holmes ever played from, or even read, music; or indeed that he had any sheet music in the house. He simply made up tunes out of his head as he went along. So much for the Bach Chaconne theory. But he had remarkable confidence in his violin's hypnotic powers.

> 'Look here, Watson, you look regularly done' [says Holmes in *The Sign of Four*]. 'Lie down there on the sofa and see if I can put you to sleep.' He took up his violin from the corner, and as I stretched myself out he began to play some low, dreamy, melodious air – his own, no doubt, for he had a remarkable gift for improvisation. I have a vague remembrance of his gaunt limbs, his earnest face, and the rise and fall of his brow. Then I seemed to float peacefully away upon a soft sea of sound, until I found myself in dreamland, with the sweet face of Mary Morstan looking down upon me.

Holmes, declares Watson in *The Red-Headed League*, '... was an enthusiastic musician, being himself not only a very capable performer, but a composer of no ordinary merit.'

So if Holmes was unable to read, let alone write, music, and was obliged to 'improvise', how would he have overcome the handicap of not knowing how to inscribe those troublesome black dots (though six decades later the Beatles did achieve a remarkable success as 'composers', albeit with the help of an army of amanuenses)?

Even more unlikely is Watson's boast that Holmes had written an important musicological treatise, a monograph entitled *The Polyphonic Motets of Lassus*. A quick check through the list of more than 500 motets known to have been composed by Roland de Lassus (1532-94) reveals that *all* are polyphonic, and they vary in scoring between three and eight voices. So the very title, 'The Polyphonic Motets of Lassus', is as tautologous as might have been, say, 'The 14-line Sonnets of Shakespeare'. Besides, Lassus would have been difficult music for Holmes to research. He played the violin only 'by ear', and was apparently unable to play the piano, even haltingly. Without being able to read music (there were no Lassus recordings then) a motet by this sixteenth-century Flemish composer would for him have been indistinguishable from, say, a Monteverdi madrigal. And besides, was it possible that there could be a respectable, middle-class Victorian house without a piano? Doyle mentions only one keyboard instrument – and that in an unpublished story – being 'idly strummed on'.

In *The Mazarin Stone* Holmes retires to his bedroom for five minutes, Watson reports, 'to try over the Hoffmann Barcarolle upon his violin.' Here he might have pretended to be reading when actually playing from memory: no one who hears Offenbach's famous Barcarolle from *Les contes d'Hoffmann* even once is likely to get that dreary tune off his mind.

Holmes and Watson diligently attended concerts and operas, and Conan Doyle took pains to lend topicality to the detective stories by mentioning real performers of the time, as well as actual London concert halls in which they appeared. Unfortunately, Holmes's demeanour during the performances they attended was not always in the best of taste. He commits the solecism of conducting the performers from his stalls, waving his hands about to the certain annoyance of others. Not even his musical hero, the celebrated Belgian violinist Pablo Sarasate, whom they heard in the St James's Hall in 1890 (as reported in *The Red-Headed League*), could avoid his unsolicited time-beating: 'All the afternoon he sat in the stalls wrapped in the most perfect happiness, gently waving his thin long fingers in time to the music ...'

The Hound of the Baskervilles has Holmes and Watson enjoying Meyerbeer's *Les Huguenots* at Covent Garden – perhaps its 200th performance, which records show was given on 20 July 1891. Watson mentions that 'the de Reszkes' were among the singers, which could probably be verified in the Covent Garden archives. They were the brothers Jean and Edouard de Reszke (whose surname was later inappropriately annexed for a particularly noxious brand of cigarette, as Lord Olivier's was later borrowed for a cigar). Watson slept peacefully through the performance; while Holmes, no doubt, used those 'thin long fingers' of his to help out the conductor.

In *A Study in Scarlet*, Holmes attends a concert, this time without Watson as sleeping partner, at which Madame Norman-Neruda performed on the violin. She, too, was a real-life performer, also known as Lady Hallé, the wife of the conductor Sir Charles Hallé. She had one thing in common with Holmes: she owned a Stradivarius, the so-called 'Ernst', named after Paganini's rival, Heinrich Ernst. That instrument was presented to her by the then Duke of Edinburgh, himself a fine violinist; whereas Holmes's instrument, if it still exists, would have to be known as 'The Tottenham Court Road Strad'. Before the concert Holmes tells Watson that Neruda's 'attack and bowing are splendid', and asks, 'what's that little thing of Chopin she plays so magnificently: "Tra-la-la-lira-lira-lay"?' Unfortunately Chopin failed to write any solo violin music (at any rate such as would have been known then), but Guy Warrack ingeniously – if not perhaps quite convincingly – fitted the syllables 'Tra-la-la-lira-lira-lay' to Chopin's F minor Nocturne. This was, of course, composed for piano, and while an arrangement for violin and piano may have existed, it would have been a highly unlikely choice for Norman-Neruda repertoire. She might, however, have appropriated Chopin's Variations on Rossini's *Non più mesta*, originally for flute and piano, and played them on the violin, though again this is most improbable.

A careless remark by Holmes himself reveals that he was not too well-informed about the difference between French and German music: 'Put your hat on and come,' he says to Watson; 'I observe that there is a good deal of German music on the programme, which is rather more to my taste than Italian or French. It is introspective, and I want to introspect. Come along!' I suppose Brahms's music might have struck him as 'introspective', though he never mentions him at all. French impressionist composers, on the other hand, *were* beginning to be heard in London at the end of the nineteenth century – and usually dismissed, though *their* music certainly was introspective.

Holmes preferred women singers to men, and contraltos to sopranos. In July 1898 he and Watson went to the Royal Albert Hall to hear 'Carina' sing. Warrack checked the annals and found that no performer of that name appeared in that hall, or indeed in London. It might have been Doyle's misremembering of Annie Louise Cary, an American mezzo-contralto. Or did he turn Cary into an affectionate nickname, 'Carina'?

Nor do we know whom Conan Doyle had in mind when, in *A Scandal in Bohemia*, he introduces an American prima donna called Irene Adler. Whoever she was in real life, Holmes tells us more about her than about most performers: for example, that she was born in New Jersey in 1858 and sang both at La Scala, Milan, and the Imperial Opera in Warsaw, was a mistress of royalty (plenty of real singers of the time filled that role) and with a voice that always beguiled the detective: a low mezzo-soprano. But no such singer seems to have existed. More research is needed: she may yet prove to have been Larry Adler's grandmother.

In addition to these 'real' musicians, many musically gifted amateurs appear in the stories. The garotter Parker, in *The Empty House*, was 'a remarkable performer upon the Jew's harp' – clearly intended to be dismissive of a popular street instrument. But Conan Doyle would not have known that it had a respectable ancestry. So much so that Beethoven's teacher Johann Albrechtsberger took it seriously enough to write a concerto for it. When Holmes, in *The Illustrious Client*, says, 'My old friend

Charlie Peace was a violin virtuoso,' but gives no further explanation, he may have meant to be sarcastic. Peace, a notorious thief, burglar and murderer, no more played the violin than he was Holmes's 'old friend': according to contemporary newspaper cuttings his instrument was actually a one-string fiddle, nicknamed a 'musical poker'. Perhaps his ill-gotten gains enabled him to buy the more sophisticated version, the Stroh violin, named after its inventor Charles Stroh, a contemporary of Sir Arthur Conan Doyle.

In *A Study in Scarlet* Holmes holds forth to Watson about the difference between a Strad and an Amati (rehashing information which Conan Doyle had probably just picked up in real life at a

WIND
BROWN, HAVING UNGUARDEDLY CONFESSED TO BEING MUSICAL, HIS FRIEND WIFFLES OFFERS TO COME AND BRING THREE OTHER FELLOWS AND PLAY SOME BEAUTIFUL FLUTE QUARTETS IN HIS ROOMS. POOR BROWN SAYS HE NEVER SAT FOR HOURS IN SUCH A THOROUGH DRAUGHT IN HIS LIFE.

(By kind permission of *Punch*)
1876

celebrated exhibition of old musical instruments in the Victoria and Albert Museum held at the time). As Watson says, 'Our meal was a merry one' – for Holmes enlivened it by discussing a variety of subjects, including Stradivarius violins. Again in *The Cardboard Box*, 'We had a pleasant little meal together, during which Holmes would talk about nothing but violins, narrating with great exultation how he had purchased his own Stradivarius, which was worth at least five hundred guineas, at a Jew broker's in the Tottenham Court Road, for fifty-five shillings.' Even at £2.75p he was done. And yet, Strad or not, it must have been the most remarkable instrument ever to come out of the Cremona workshops; because when, in *The Norwood Builder*, during a fit of exasperation, Holmes 'flung down the instrument' into a corner, it came to no harm. It was 'made of mahogany'. Solid, no doubt.

Mr and Mrs Korngold disagree

Erich Wolfgang Korngold (1897-1957) was one of the many Czech musicians who during the course of two eventful centuries helped to give the Austrians their reputation for being a musical people. He was born to a Jewish musical family in what was then Brünn, a place the Czechs have always called Brno. Korngold's cantata *Gold* was heard in 1907, when he was barely ten, and his ballet *Der Schneemann* (The Snowman), written at the age of 11, was professionally produced in Vienna in 1910.

He was hailed as a second Mozart, an accolade not lightly given in Vienna, but both Puccini and Richard Strauss concurred that he was a boy genius. The advent of Nazism in 1933 in Germany effectively put an end to his Austrian career while at the same time opening up a much more lucrative one. For, in the mid-1930s, he went to Hollywood with the operatic and theatrical producer Max Reinhardt, and the annexation of Austria meant that Korngold was unable to return home. He stayed in the United States for the rest of his life, and devoted most of his energies to writing film scores, getting Oscars for films such as *Anthony Adverse* and *The Adventures of Robin Hood* – classics of their kind and role models for much of the film music that followed. They earned him millions – and also, of course, the jealousy of many musicians, who declared he had sold his soul to the devil, and that his film music was 'more corn than gold'.

Korngold's music is now gradually being revived and reassessed, and there exists a flourishing Korngold Society. His early successes may have been helped a little by the fact that his father Julius was an influential Viennese music critic and Frau Korngold a very pushy mother. In 1910, at a rehearsal of the 13-year-old composer's Piano Trio, little Erich was sitting between his parents. His mother called out, 'Too *fast!*' Herr Korngold said, 'No. It's too *slow!*' Erich piped up and said, '*I* think it's just right.' Whereupon both parents rounded on him, '*You* shut up!'

Stravinsky and Vaughan Williams want six-fingered harpists

Since the Middle Ages players of wind and string instruments have drawn up fingering charts and tablatures – easy-to-read diagrams indicating the position of the fingers for different notes. Composers, too, are meant to study these, so that they do not write notes beyond an instrument's range. There are also handbooks on orchestration, some by famous composers like Berlioz, Rimsky-Korsakov and Frederick Corder, who passed on their experience to students. Unfortunately, many modern composers have not bothered about such things – just as students of English no longer learn grammar or syntax.

Every orchestral player rehearsing some modern work is at one time or another faced with an instrumental impossibility; and if the composer is present and asked how it might be played he will usually shrug off the question, saying that free expression is paramount, and the mechanics secondary. Again a parallel suggests itself with the spelling and grammar of English.

Orchestral players are resigned to this. They quietly fake the passage, and unless it is a solo no one is usually the wiser. Harpists in particular have long been used to 'cooking' the parts written for them. Many of even the most distinguished composers believe that playing the harp is like playing the piano: five fingers on each hand. In truth, five-note chords are impossible on the instrument, as harpists do not use their fourth fingers: little fingers are literally too little to be of any use.

Nevertheless, Igor Stravinsky and Ralph Vaughan Williams were among numerous composers who lived long and productive lives and wrote much music – but laboured under this misapprehension. Both habitually demanded five notes from each of the harpist's hands. The wonder is that their friends never mentioned it: for example, the celebrated harpist Maria Korchinska, who knew Stravinsky well and might have said to him in their native Russian, 'Look here, Igor, how do you expect me to play this?' Or the long-serving harpist of the Hallé Orchestra, Charles Cockerill, who could have buttonholed Vaughan Williams.

Gustav Mahler and Benjamin Britten habitually wrote low notes which are not available on wind instruments because they are either too high or too low. In direct response to these blunders low-B extensions have become commonplace on flutes (though not extensions going down to B flat, for which Mahler also asked); and a few piccolos, specifically called ottavinos, go down to C sharp and C, two semitones below their normal range. Why did no one tell these composers? Anton Webern wrote a bottom G flat for the violin, a semitone lower than its lowest string. The player asked him how it should be played, as there was no time to tune the string down. According to the violinist, George Mayer Marton (who was present and told me the story), Webern replied, 'You do not *play* it – you *think* it,' and accordingly he marked the note 'pensato'.

Benjamin Britten makes several utterly impossible demands in his works, such as rapid alternations of notes as a tremolo effect. But anyone asking him, at rehearsal, to be allowed to change a passage slightly so as to make it playable would receive short shrift (he was an extremely touchy man).

Perhaps all these composers model themselves on Beethoven who, when asked about a passage his violinist friend Ignaz Schuppanzigh told him was impossible, retorted 'What do I care about your miserable violin?'

Band and contraband

The gangsters' trick of hiding machine guns in fiddle cases may be a modern cliché but an interesting variation on it was played during the years of skyjacking of the 1970s and 1980s, when an over-zealous (and possibly dyslectic) airport policeman searched the instrument cases of a handful of members of the London Philharmonic Orchestra travelling on their own. It turned out that he had misread the initials LPO as PLO.

Between 1598 and 1603 the English artist, architect and stage designer Inigo Jones travelled widely in Europe, absorbing and assimilating the latest in foreign tastes. There he heard a theorbo (a bass lute) being played in Florence, where it had been invented by Antonio Naldi in 1592 and decided to bring one back to England: he should have brought back two, hoping that they might breed, as the city councillor said when he suggested importing two gondolas from Venice.

Such an enormous, big-bellied instrument had never before been seen in the country and when Jones got to Dover a jittery customs man confiscated it, supposing it to be 'some engine brought from popish countries to destroy the king'.

Returning from abroad with foreign objects is an old orchestral pastime. When Sir John Barbirolli and the Hallé Orchestra left Manchester for a long South American tour in 1968 the orchestral instruments weighed two tons. Just before the orchestra's return, a worried orchestra manager announced that the instruments now weighed three tons.

MODERN CRAZES – THE LAST THING IN MUSICAL PRODIGIES – THE BABY BOTTESINI.

(By kind permission of *Punch*)

1887

Practice makes perfect

Practice is important for instrumentalists. It preserves and develops their sight-reading skills and stamina, and keeps muscle-and-ear co-ordination alert. But many older and experienced orchestral players, once they know the repertoire, feel they can get along with a minimum of practice. The bandrooms and lockers of contract orchestras which have their base in a concert hall are usually full of instruments which hardworking players leave there from one concert to the next, though some claim they keep a second instrument at home for practising on. When Fred Devlin retired after many years as principal trombonist of the Royal Liverpool Philharmonic, he was given a small party, then made his farewells, retrieved his trombone from the locker and went home. On his arrival, his wife opened the front door, looked down at the curiously shaped trombone case and said, 'Er – what's *that* you've got there, dear?'

Making a domino

Playing a wrong note in an orchestra is simply called – playing a wrong note. But the most common orchestral blunder has its own name – domino. A domino is an obvious false entry: playing the right note at the wrong moment. The worst kind is made in silence, when no one else is playing: everyone notices it; and a red face with a sheepish look reveals who made it. One of the unwritten rules of orchestral etiquette dictates that no player turns round, or even looks at, the culprit: 'eyes front' is the order of the day.

But a domino-making player also gets the blame (and a red face) when he is following a mistaken lead from the conductor. Sir Thomas Beecham once beat an extra bar at the end of a piece – and only a conductor can make a *silent* domino. On that occasion he sought out the timpanist afterwards and said with a twinkle, 'You must know that in instances like this it is the duty of the percussion to support the conductor.'

Indeed, two conductors' dominoes took place in a BBC studio during two separate live broadcasts (in which I took part). One was at the end of Gustav Holst's *The Perfect Fool*, in which the conductor, John Hopkins, beat a fortissimo chord one bar too early in what should have been a silence. Only the timpanist followed him. On another occasion Sir Malcolm Arnold was conducting one of his own symphonies with the same orchestra and beat an extra bar at the end of the quiet-slow movement. On this occasion nobody played, as they had nothing to play.

The origin of the word is obscure, but the English singer Sir Charles Santley (1834-1922), in his book *Student and Singer* (1892), reveals that it was already current in the middle of the nineteenth century; 'I did not notice the bar's rest before the Amen, and performed a solo, which called forth some witty remark from [the conductor Sir Julius] Benedict about the future of the singer who made the "domino".'

In the game of dominoes, 'making the domino' means to finish first, which may give a clue to the implications of an orchestral player's jumping the gun. Benedict was originally German, so it might have been a word he brought to England, but Avgerinos's *Musikerjargon* (a dictionary of German musicians' jargon) does not include it. In orchestral slang a place in the score where dominoes are likely to occur, eg, a series of isolated chords coming at regular and irregular intervals (as in Tchaikovsky's *Romeo and Juliet*), is known as 'Domino Corner'. The *Oxford English Dictionary* defines it in erroneously general terms, as simply 'An error in performance', quoting from Santley, as well as the *Penguin Music Magazine* of December 1946, in which an orchestral player is quoted: 'One can get away with a domino once – even thrice, but then someone starts to say: "Poor Blank, he is beginning to slip".'

A disaster at San Carlo Opera House

The German writer J W von Archenholz, whose account of *A Trip to Italy*, was published in London in 1791, relates a musical disaster which, he claims, befell a castrato singer in Naples in about 1765:

> A very peculiar accident happened a few years ago to a singer of the name of Balani. This man was born without any visible signs of those parts which are taken out in castration. He was, therefore, looked upon as a true-born castrato; an opinion, which was even confirmed by his voice. He learned music, and sung for several years upon the theatre with great applause. One day, he exerted himself so uncommonly in singing an arietta, that all of a sudden those parts, which had so long been concealed by nature, dropped into their proper place. The singer from this very instant lost his voice ... and with it lost every prospect of a future subsistence.

A disaster in the Liverpool Philharmonic Hall

The baton may be the only silent musical instrument (even the practice piano makes a gentle clatter of keys) but it can bring down a whole performance: one bar with the wrong number of beats in it, or a confusion between down beats and side beats, can make a performance collapse. Even if the players are right, the conductor can mislead them into going wrong.

During the late 1940s the pianist Gordon Green was engaged to play two works for piano and orchestra with the Liverpool Philharmonic Orchestra, conducted by Richard Austin: Liszt's *Totentanz* and Rawsthorne's Piano Concerto No 1. One was scheduled for the first half, the other for the second, after the interval. The concert began with an overture. Having played this, the players opened their copies of the Rawsthorne (orchestral librarians always place the music in the correct sequence). Gordon Green entered, acknowledged the applause and sat down to play the Rawsthorne concerto. But Austin had the wrong score open, and thought it was the Liszt in the first half, so he began conducting it, with a firm signal to the timpanist – and by a lucky coincidence both start with the kettledrums alone. The timpanist embarked on the Rawsthorne, and the orchestra tried to, but the conductor was beating the Liszt *Totentanz*. For a short time there was chaos, until Austin stopped the orchestra, turned round and said to the audience, 'Ladies and gentlemen, I'm sorry. I was conducting the wrong concerto.'

Amid much merriment the conductor restarted and all went well. The initial mishap came as a welcome relief for Gordon Green who, although a fine player, suffered so much from stage-fright that he was physically ill for days before each performance. As there is nothing so tension breaking as a comic incident before one has to play it helped him to settle down, though he eventually accepted that he was not a performer and concentrated on teaching, with John Ogdon, John McCabe, Martin Tirimo and many others as pupils.

A not unrelated blunder broke the ice – and probably also the spell – for Green's teacher, Egon Petri, because it dissolved both audience and performers into laughter. Petri (Green told me) had been booked to play a concert containing two Beethoven concertos: No 4 in G major and No 3 in C minor. The conductor and the soloist (Green could not recall who the former was) entered together, bowed, and went to their respective stations. On the rostrum the conductor found open the score of the G major concerto, which starts with the piano alone. Petri sat down, adjusted his piano stool and, believing he was playing the C minor concerto first, folded his hands in his lap and smiled up at the conductor to signal that he was comfortable and ready for the opening orchestral introduction. The conductor, his arms by his side, thought Petri would start the G major – smiled and nodded to the pianist; who smiled and nodded back. The mutual nodding-smiling-bowing routine (After you, no after *you*!) went on for some time until the players realized what had happened and the orchestra started to giggle. Petri got up and the conductor stepped down, and after a quick conference they decided which concerto came first.

But when performers reach their anecdotage they sometimes misremember details, even of incidents in which they took a leading part. The pianist Cyril Smith recounts in his autobiography *Three Hands* how a conductor once dropped his baton into his piano while he was playing Rachmaninov's Piano Concerto No 2. It bounced up and down on the strings, temporarily turning the piano into a kind of percussion instrument, until a viola player got up and fished it out. That was the story as far as it went but Ronald Settle, another distinguished

Teacher: AND WHAT DOES FF MEAN?
Pupil (after mature deliberation): FUMP-FUMP.

(By kind permission of *Punch*)
1920

pianist, who was present, later reminded Smith that he was (for once) not playing his favourite 'Rack Two' but the more rarely played Weber *Konzertstück*. The moral is – if you intend to write your memoirs, make notes while events are fresh in your mind.

Advice to piano pupils

Always wash your hands before
Fingering the virgin score;
Never park your boiled sweets, please,
On the clean piano keys;
Practise scales? Of course, you must –
Pedalled softly, though, we trust!
Do not, with a single digit,
Pick out tunes that make us fidget;
Lest the noxious habit grow,
Curb the crude arpeggio;
              AND
If your progress piles up doubts,
Chuck it, child, and join the Scouts.

Allan M Laing

And from the examiner's notebook ...

The following amusing incident happened the other day at Burnley in connection with the examinations of the College of Violinists, now in progress. Youth of about 14, up for examination for graduate, played fairly well and answered questions put to him rather smartly:

Examiner: Now, please, tell me the relative minor of the scale of G minor.

Candidate (somewhat puzzled): B, sir.

Examiner: B what? (after a while repeating the question, tapping the desk with his pencil)

Secretary (who happened to be in the room, overlooking the paperwork of the candidates, muttering to himself): Be quick!

Candidate (quite loud): Be quick, sir.

The Violin Times 15 July 1894

Lully wrote quite a few foke songs.

Vaughn Williams is another one who is very fond of folk melodies in queer keys.

Bach married twice and had 20 children and no dought this was an influence in his composition of varying moods.

Bach had two wives and 20 children and he kept a spinster in the attic for practising on.

Bach finally wrecked his piano with trying to make it sound louder.

Handel wrote forwards, Bach wrote backwards.

Plaingsong was written down by the Neumes.

Later came the idea of counterpoint and a period came when very heavy contrary motion was used.

Emotion plus the voice gave song.

Organum was the art of being organized.

A virginal is a piano that has never been played on.

The harpsichord was used to add small trimmings to the musical form.

Though the madrigal proper was contrupuntal in style, the ayre incorporated harmonies of sorts.

Enthusiast: WE SHALL HEAR MORE OF THIS YOUNG MAN.
Sufferer: NOT TONIGHT I HOPE.

(By kind permission of *Punch*)
1909

There are three distinct forms in music – the simple, the classic, and the decadent.

Mendelssohn's Hymn of Praise was written to commemorate the anniversary of printing.

The modern composers seem to have run out of nice melodies so they rely on the percussion to do its stuff.

Peter Grimes is a tone poem by Richard Strauss.

Wagner wrote Tristan and Essoldo.

8

Songs my mother never taught me

Caramel cream, to music

Words are easily forgotten, and so are tunes; but when heard together the combination tends to stick in the mind. Noël Coward's 'potency of cheap music' refers more to the texts than the music: the more foolish the words the more stubbornly they stick in the memory. Louis XV had a wonderful chef but he had a memory like a sieve, and kept forgetting some of the ingredients, until he versified the recipes and set them to music, a collection of which he eventually published as the world's first musical cookery book. Here is an example, a recipe for Caramel Cream:

> Eight egg-yolks, flour,
> Cinnamon, lemon-rind,
> Sugar and a modicum of salt
> A pint of milk.
>
> Cook it all in the oven
> And make a caramel
> In a silver dish
> Which you must take note of.
>
> Pour this cream into it
> Stirring lightly meanwhile,
> Cook it promptly
> With extreme care.
>
> When it is cool
> Glaze it on top
> With sugar
> And a red-hot shovel.

How to ruin a tune

Music teachers have used this method of adding mnemonic jingles to instrumental music so as to make pupils remember them. It works but the trouble is that for the musically more sensitive some sublime tune may be ruined for ever. The American music teacher Sigmund Spaeth went so far as to claim that there was no such thing as a purely *musical* memory. Tunes, he said baldly, can be recalled only by an association with words – even symphonies. Haydn, Mozart, Beethoven and the rest provided the tunes, Professor Spaeth the words; and in 1936 he published a whole book of musical *aides-memoires* entitled *Great Symphonies: How to Recognize and Remember Them*. In this way he manages to remove any surprise from Haydn's 'Surprise' Symphony by giving the joke away:

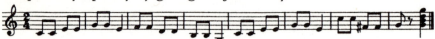

Papa Hadyn wrote this tune, and a chord is coming soon, It will be a   big surprise,   Open   sleepy   eyes!   Bang!

and in the 'Clock' Symphony makes absolutely certain no one can possibly miss the allusion:

Tick tock tick tock! Hear the tick tock sound on high, The clock is telling ev'ryone how time goes by.

Mozart's late G minor Symphony, with its brooding, anguished opening, is to Spaeth 'a very happy tune, full of laughter and fun':

With a laugh and a smile like a sunbeam,   And a   face that is glad with a funbeam,   We can start on our way very   gaily,.   Singing tunes from a symphony   daily;   And if Mozart could but hear us,   He would wave his hat and cheer us coming down the scale, all   hale   and   strong   in   song,   all   hale and strong in   song.

Beethoven's first symphony starts off by trailing the succeeding eight:

Here's number one, and you know there will be nine before the great Beethoven's done.

In No 5 he harps on the 'Fate' story:

I am your Fate! Come, let me in!

For the Ninth, Spaeth attempted a translation of Schiller's 'Ode to Joy', but could not resist adding words of his own to the rest of the Symphony, for example the Scherzo:

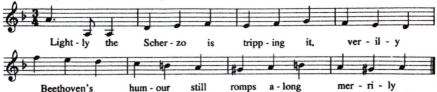

Light - ly the Scher - zo is tripp - ing it, ver - il - y

Beethoven's hum - our still romps a - long mer - ri - ly

When someone said to Brahms that the 'big tune' of the last movement of his first symphony reminded him of Beethoven's Ninth, he replied, 'Any fool can see that.' It takes a special fool to turn it into this:

When Brahms marches on - ward, each loy - al heart keeps time, His

tones ring out nob - ly, with me - lo - dy sub - lime We

join in sing - ing and bring - ing our ring - ing praise to

Brahms the great at Heaven's gate, With green palms and loud Psalms to Brahms.

Ebenezer Prout makes Bach sound silly

To most music lovers the name Ebenezer Prout is familiar from the widely used edition (many a time misprinted as 'Sprouts Edition') of Handel's *Messiah*, which he furnished with added nineteenth-century orchestration. His editing was scholarly and sound, as he was a distinguished Handel scholar in his time; and his re-orchestration is largely based on that by Mozart – which did not save him from the condemnation of the 'authentic' music lobby. Prout (who was born in 1835 and died in 1909) also wrote numerous excellent academic treatises on harmony, counterpoint, fugue and musical form, which were gradually superseded and gained him the reputation of a staid Victorian Professor of Music. He may have been a little dotty, but never stuffy, and students enjoyed his lectures. During the 1950s some survivors came forward to report that, far from being dry as dust, he taught them about Bach's fugues in a way no one else could, and that he made them sing words to the Forty-eight, of which some kept complete lists.

Fugue 2, Book 1

John Sebastian Bach sat upon a tack, but he soon got up again with a howl!

Fugue 7

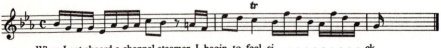

When I get aboard a channel steamer I begin to feel si - - - - - - - - - ck.

Fugue 20

On a bank of mud in the River Nile, upon a summer morning a

little hippopotamus was eating bread and jam.

Not all his fellow academics were amused by his treatment of Bach, and his contemporary Sir Charles Stanford replied by parodying in the Prout style Bach's great G minor Organ Fugue (BWV 542):

Oh Ebenezer Prout you are a funny man, you make Bach sound as silly as you can.

English as she is sung

Translating vocal music, whether folk songs or *Lieder*, whether a simple French *chanson* or a grand opera, is a specialized art which many attempt but few have conquered. Andrew Porter's translation of Wagner's Ring cycle and Arthur Jacobs's of *L'incoronazione di Poppea* are rare masterpieces, being both readable and singable. That they may not always be audible is not the translators' fault, and it almost seems as if anglicizers of the old school relied on the assumption that their work would not be heard; and that therefore it didn't much matter anyway.

Vocal music seldom follows the same syllabic course as poetry, so why do translators insist on rhymes, instead of concentrating on the sense? After all, many poets use unrhymed 'verse' that neither rhymes nor scans. Yet in translated texts (as in pre-twentieth-century poetry) 'eye rhymes' proliferate, with words that look the same but sound different: 'grove/prove/love'. Translators go through all sorts of linguistic contortions to get a rhyme. An English version of Puccini's *Tosca* has the opening lines,

Ha! I have baulked them!
Dread Imagination
Made me quake
With uncalled-for Perturbation!

– peppered with exclamation marks as printed here. It sets the tone of the whole translation, by William Beatty-Kingston (1837-1900). In Verdi's *Falstaff*, too, he put into the eponymous hero's mouth words you will not find in Shakespeare:

How I'll bamboozle him, neatly, featly!
The animal, I'll worry him!
The imbecile, I'll flurry him!

If you can actually distinguish the words during the course of a performance in an English translation of Beethoven's *Fidelio* – which is still being sung – you may hear Leonora sing

My Purpose shall not stagger
Till his Heart doth sheathe my dagger ...

– in other words she would like to stab him. Rocco, the jailer, is made to sing to Leonora:

You tremble, you fear some thing will *harm* thee?

She replies,

I'm only cold.

To which he replies, quick as a flash,

Quick then to work and *warm* thee.

To make matters worse, when she picks up a sack he sings,

What a lot of weight
you have to carry.

Which is not a nice thing to sing to a lady. Such rhymes-at-any-cost obsession makes it only a matter of time before we have Rodolfo telling Mimi in Puccini's *La Bohème* not that her tiny hand is frozen but 'Your midget digit is frigid'. Charles Kenney's translation of *Aida* is a veritable goldmine for happy infelicities, like

> Torrents of blood shall crimson flow
> Grimly the foe stands gloating.
> Seest thou, from Death's dark gulf below,
> Shades of the dead upfloating.

Carl Maria von Weber thought he was being wise to engage an English writer to make him an English version of Wieland's *Oberon* – not a translation but a new libretto. But, James Robinson Planché (1796-1880), who was clearly a poet *manqué*, managed to write original lines that *sound* like a bad translation:

> Hark, lady, hark! On the terrace near
> The tread of the harem guard I hear
> And lo! thy slaves that hither hie
> Show that the hour of rest is nigh.

However, no one can blame Planché for the fact that the meaning of words is constantly changing. So when the heroine, Reiza, sang 'Thou art an awful sight!' she was not addressing a fellow member of the cast but the sea, of which she was in awe; and when she sees a ship on the horizon and sings, 'Oh transport!' she means happiness, not the hope of hitching a passage. In the English version of Verdi's *Simon Boccanegra*, as sung by the Welsh National Opera, as Gabriele tries to stab the Doge, Amelia intervenes with the homely words, 'Are you quite mad?'

Not only opera. In both Verdi's and Mozart's Requiems, in an old Boosey edition, the passage about the last trumpet, *Tuba mirum spargens sonum*, is given in English as 'Hark, the trumpet sounds appalling!' The *inter oves* section, the part where the Latin Mass separates the sheep from the goats, has:

> With Thy sheep, Lord deign to mate me,
> From the He-goats separate me ...

which is varied in another edition to

In thy favoured sheep's position
Keep me from the goat's condition.

In Handel's opera *Hercules* you can expect the Handelian repetition of syllables to plod along for many bars, so that no translator is required to follow: 'You creep, you creep, you creep, you creep, you creep away.' The opera also contains the now rather ambiguous line, when Hercules is asked to drop his weapon, of 'Resign thy club.'

At the end of Donizetti's *Lucia di Lammermoor*, the heroine, Lucy, stands over the body of her lover with a bloodstained dagger in her hand. In one version the chorus comments on the action with the immortal lines:

In her hand a weapon grasping,
Even his, who lies there gasping!

For a drink? In another opera on a classical subject, the hero, mortally wounded, is about to expire, when someone calls for a stretcher, singing, 'Bring on the bier.' Benjamin Britten, in one of his children's operas, *The Little Sweep*, has the poor boy chimneysweep pleading with his master, '*Please* don't send me up again!' He does, mercilessly. Britten's need to have children in his operas is made a little less wicked by the fact that in some respects he was himself an innocent (and like many a child possessed a large streak of viciousness). How else but in innocence could he have written, or sanctioned, some of the double-edged lines in his libretti? For example, in *Owen Wingrave*, originally a television opera with a libretto by Myfanwy Piper, based on a story by Henry James and dealing with pacifism and cowardice, he has Owen (a part created in 1973 by Benjamin Luxon) trying to prove his manhood by promising to spend the night alone in a locked and haunted room. As expected, like all Britten's heroes, he fails the crucial test of masculinity. In the original libretto his supposed girlfriend Kate was at first required to sing the lines, 'I will not marry you if you can't stick it out', until Janet Baker pointed out that she could not sing the lines and keep a straight face. (Owen does in the end stick it out but dies in the room, of fright.)

In Schubert's song 'Wohin?' almost every English version translates *Ich hört ein Bächlein rauschen* as either 'I heard a brooklet rushing' or 'I heard a brooklet gushing'. The German *rauschen* means *neither* rushing nor gushing, but the translator obviously thought it sounded as if it *should*. In the event it is usually only the singer who gushes. (By the same token of sound-instead-of-sense Schumann's *Frauenliebe* may be translated as 'women's lib'.) *Rauschen* is untranslatable in a single word. It is a combination of trickling and purling if applied to water; rustling if to leaves or silk, and murmuring if detected (medically) in the heart or ears: when Beethoven complained of *rauschen* in his ears he meant a tinnitus. Such confusions and misunderstandings are legion. In Verdi's *Un ballo in maschera* the line *sento l'orme de' passi spietati* is given in English as 'I hear footprints', when foot*steps* might have made more sense (Italian *sentir* is a multi-purpose word implying hearing, seeing or feeling).

Schubert's '*Irrlicht*' (Will o' the Wisp), the ninth song in the song cycle *Die Winterreise*, begins *In die tiefsten Felsengründe*. Working with A H Fox Strangways, Sir Steuart Wilson, singer and a *quondam* BBC director of music, transformed this into 'On a mountain bog I blundered'. The same collaboration produced an English version of *Am Feierabend*, which in the nonsense stakes could hardly be bettered:

> O that I'd a giant's inches
> And could guide the pond'rous winches!

When Schubert's friend, the poet Eduard von Bauernfeld, translated 'Who is Sylvia?' for him to set to music, he turned the question into not 'who' but *Was ist Sylvia?* (What is Sylvia?), telescoping the first line with the second part of Shakespeare's second question, 'What is she?' Fortunately here there is no need to translate it back into English, as most of the original words can be made to fit the music. Only when the lines are spoken can verbal inflexions be applied – and with the appropriate timing can even be changed at will, eg, 'Who is? Sylvia? Whaaat! IS she?'

HUSH-SH-SH-SH!
Angelina (who has been chatting agreeably ever since the music began): OH,
DON'T YOU DOTE ON PART SINGING, CAPTAIN EDWIN!
Captain Edwin: I DO INDEED – PART SINGING AND PART TALKING, YOU KNOW!
(By kind permission of *Punch*)
1870

A Japanese choir performs in Oxford

Programmes, too, can suffer in translation, as these programme notes on English sea shanties can testify:

Swansea Town. March in light mode singing goodbye to Swansea Town in Wales, hoping to see once more.

Haul Away Joe. Producing choir effect in proceed per canonem in old style.

Brow the Man Down. Famous English Shanty with bass solo accompanied by choir in vigor mood.

What shall we Do with the Drunken Sailor. The oldest English shanty of comic mood, expressing crew's optimistic nature.

Elgar, his sheds and other linguistic confusions

When the young (therefore not yet Sir) Edward Elgar worked in the Worcester county lunatic asylum, he composed a number of charming trifles for wind quintet. He played the bassoon in them, his brother Frank the flute. Officially, Elgar was the asylum bandmaster but he was probably expected also to act as a part-time attendant. He called these pieces 'sheds' and this has led to the invention of a romantic myth that 'the young Elgar rehearsed with his quintet in a garden shed' (just as Mahler had a 'composing-hut' built in the garden of every holiday house he occupied: a romantic notion but a false one). Elgar was an avid reader of old English texts, including Holinshed's *Chronicles*, and would therefore have known that a *schede* or *schediasm*, is an extemporized work, a superficial jotting; and anyway he himself said he composed the 'sheds' in the asylum chapel's organ loft, during long and boring sermons, while looking forward to the wind-quintet parties. No one has so far found that mythical garden shed or better, all three, as he called the pieces Shed No 1, Shed No 2, Shed No 3, etc.

The title of Elgar's *Cockaigne* overture also sprang from his fascination with words, and has also led to etymological blunders. A foreign paper in the early 1900s invented the dangerous fantasy that in it 'Elgar describes the ravages which this dreadful drug wrought on unfortunate Londoners addicted to it'. Prophetic perhaps, but doubly ludicrous. Cockaigne, in various spellings, *has* been facetiously applied to cockneys since 1824 (strictly those born within sound of the Bow Bells) and the overture *is* subtitled 'In London Town'; but in its older sense, which Elgar must have known, cockaigne means the same country as *Schlaraffenland*, described in the last movement of Mahler's Symphony No 4 as 'a child's vision of heaven'. Here no one needs to work and heaven-sent, ready-roasted chickens fly through the air (no doubt cut into bite-sized nuggets) straight into the beneficiaries' mouths – the ultimate in take-away deliveries on the Welfare State. The *Oxford English Dictionary* traces the word to the ancient French *coquaigne*, Italian *cuccagna*, and even the German *Kuchen* – all related to cooking and eating, and (without even mentioning the German *Schlaraffenland*) calls cockaigne 'the country where good things drop of themselves into the mouth'.

In Jerrold Northrop Moore's *Elgar, a Creative Life* the author says that 'Somniferous', the title of one of Elgar's 'shed' pieces, was a word the composer invented. Not so. Elgar, being an habitual player with words, would have checked his *Oxford English Dictionary* and found that Thomas Dekker wrote, in 1602, about '... a true somniferous potion'. The word was also used by Dickens in 1837, as well as by other writers, to describe the sleep-inducing effects of alcohol.

A linguistic confusion 1996-style?

And as our tribute to Yehudi Menuhin's 80th birthday, we'll be looking at some of the world's most glamorous grans.

Anthea Turner, GMTV breakfast show

The life of a Rhinemaiden

Hubert Parry, just down from the Royal Academy of Music, went to Bayreuth to sample the Wagnerian atmosphere. His former principal, Sir George MacFarren, sent him a farewell letter on 12 August 1876:

> I am sorry you are going to Bayreuth, for every presence there gives countenance to the monstrous self-inflation. The principle of the thing is bad, the means for its realization preposterous. An earthquake would be good that would swallow up the spot and everybody on it, so I wish you away. Yours, with kindest regards,
>
> G A Macfarren

When Richard Wagner died in Venice in 1883 the Wagner industry went into a higher gear, as this news item indicates:

> The gondola in which Wagner took the air every day has been bought for his widow, and sent to Bayreuth. For the table at which the master used to sit in the afternoon, listening to the military band in the Piazza di San Marco, 300 francs has been offered to the owner, who, however, declines to part with it. Another curious relic, purchased, it is stated, by some hero-worshippers, is the railway truck in which the body was taken from Venice to Bayreuth.

The Watch on the Rhine

A life of a Rhinemaiden isn't so hot
    As it looks from the back of the stalls;
We do, it is true, get about quite a lot,
    But the view's much the same, and it palls.

Each performance we're cased from the toes to the waist
    In long piscatorial tails,
Then we're launched from the wings on innumerable strings
    Like a school of benevolent whales.

It isn't much fun to be twiddled around,
    Going Sir Thomas knows where,
Suspended at least thirty feet from the ground,
    It's hard to be Naiad-may-care!

We strive with our arms to display all the charms
    Of sirens who lounge upon rocks,
But our legs are congealed and our bosoms concealed
    In the most unprovocative frocks.

It's a bore to be mouthing like moribund cods
    As we're dazzled, dizzily swung,
While beneath us, obscured from the gallery gods,
    The genuine artists give tongue.

It makes us feel sick when we see Alberich
    Through a shimmering eau-de-Rhine curtain,
And a bird's-view of Fricka just makes us feel sicker –
    Of that we are perfectly certain.

At the end of the night we're surprised we're alive,
    For, controlled by invisible winches,
We are forced like recalcitrant penguins to dive,
    Avoiding each other by inches.

We are plagued by the thought that our fins may get caught,
   Or our heavenly workings may jam,
Though we don't want to fuss, it's not happy for us
   To be hung like Virginia ham.

Consider the Years, Virginia Graham,
1946

And for good measure

Perhaps this is what a young music student had in mind when he
wrote in his exam 'Wagner usually introduced some normal love
interest for good measure'?

> The curate sitting near me at the last Leeds Festival was a
> touching example of the music lover who doesn't know but is
> anxious to learn. When Miss Edyth Walker and Mr John
> Coates had finished the great duet from the first act of
> *Götterdämmerung* our curate said to the lady next to him, 'Was
> Siegfried *engaged* to Brynhilda?' I could hardly be restrained
> from rushing up to this priceless person with open arms; I
> wanted to take him home with me and keep him as a pet.

Birmingham Post,
1915

Butterfly's baby

'Never appear with children or animals', wise old actors say – and
the same advice holds good for opera singers. A variation on this
theme occurs in Mosco Carner's biography of Giacomo Puccini.
Tito Ricordi, a member of the old Italian family which published
Puccini's operas, was in charge of a production in around 1910 of

Madama Butterfly at the Manchester Opera House, when he discovered to his dismay that the Lord Chamberlain's regulations did not permit the appearance on stage of a child, let alone a baby.

Even without licensing justices and their restrictive regulations Butterfly's offspring has always presented a problem. A doll is probably the best alternative to a real baby (which might scream its head off at any moment), and modern technology can doubtless equip a doll with a machine that makes noises which will not disrupt the proceedings. Pictures of earlier productions often suggest a quite unrealistic delay between the baby's birth and its mother's decision to kill herself, with children of six or seven (depending on local child-labour regulations) being dandled on her knee. In Manchester no child was available, so Ricordi in desperation engaged a dwarf: 'This worked splendidly for several performances until one night, at the point of the action at which Butterfly embraces the child, the midget was overcome by a feeling all too human in this situation and responded to his 'mother's' affectionate gesture with most unfilial passion. *Se non è vero è ben trovato!*' But then opera demands of spectators all suspension of disbelief. How else could audiences have accepted a 65-year-old Mimi, in the form – and shape – of Adelina Patti?

Words to watch

According to Nicholas Slonimsky's *Lectionary of Music*, German productions of Puccini's *Madama Butterfly* sometimes change the name of the heroine's seducer, Lieutenant Pinkerton, because it is too close in sound to the German word *pinkeln*, which means to urinate; and Russian-language performances before Portuguese audiences of Mussorgsky's *Boris Godunov* are obliged to amend the tsar's loudly declaimed injunction *karai!* because in their language it is like shouting 'prick'.

The first entry of the solo baritone to the words *Tu rex!* (Thou, the king) in Dvořák's *Te Deum* is inevitably heard by English speakers as 'Durex'; while in Haydn's *Stabat Mater* the 'urgent shout' (as the composer's biographer Karl Geiringer called it) of the full chorus to the staccato word *Fac* also tends to be misunderstood.

Caruso 'insults' Mrs Graham in the monkey house

In November 1906 the front pages of New York newspapers led with the sensational headline TENOR CARUSO ARRESTED. Beneath this, in smaller capitals, WOMAN SAYS HE INSULTED HER IN CENTRAL PARK ZOO, and then, in the informative manner of the multi-decker headlines of those days, 'Policeman Grabbed Him and Led Him From the Monkey House to the Station – All a Mistake cries the Singer'. The news item began, breathlessly:

> Mrs Hannah Graham and her little son were in the monkey house in Central Park yesterday afternoon just before five o'clock. Mrs Graham and the boy were leaning on the railing in front of the cage when a short stout man of very dark complexion stood close to Mrs Graham. A plainclothes man, James J Kane, is attached to the Arsenal station. His special business it is to see that women in the park are not annoyed. Standing at the back of the room he noticed the woman and little boy and kept his eye also on the 'foreign-looking man' as Kane described him later. Kane saw that the woman appeared to be disturbed, and finally when the woman wheeled round on the man at her side with a very red face, and said, 'See here, what are you doing?' Kane got busy. He ran over to the railing and grabbed the man by the arm, saying to the woman, 'Do you want to make a complaint against this man?' 'I certainly do', said Mrs Graham. 'He has insulted me.'

Caruso at first claimed it had all been a mistake, then tried to pull rank: 'I am Enrico Caruso, the opera singer'; after which he pretended to speak no English; and then complained of feeling unwell. The resulting court case topped the news pages for months, revealing all kinds of strange developments – except one: what Caruso had actually *done*. Probably nothing more than crudely attempting to chat up a woman; or perhaps he was encouraged by the male monkeys (who tend to be even more uninhibited in showing their desires than male Italians) and used it as a conversation-opener with Mrs Graham. His friend Giacomo Puccini, who also tried to get off with any woman he fancied, claimed that Caruso had been set up, that it was a plot to disrupt the production of *La Bohème*, for which the tenor had gone to New York: 'It is my belief that the whole thing was a put-up job by some hostile impresario,' Puccini wrote to his London mistress Sybil Seligman on 20 November 1906. In spite of the fact that Mrs Graham refused to appear in court, and had apparently given a false name and address, Caruso was found guilty and fined. Seligman's son Vincent wrote, 'For many years "monkey-house" jokes vied in popularity with mothers-in-law, kippers, landladies and the rest of the stock-in-trade of the music-hall comedian.' Perhaps the strangest fact to emerge from this extraordinary case is that in the New York of 1908 someone could still be singled out as 'a foreign-looking man'.

Other musicians brush with the law

Caruso was historically in good company. Bach was arrested for brawling with students, having picked a fight with a bassoonist by saying his tone was like that of a goat; Schubert for alleged subversive activities (not for homosexuality as a posthumous 'outer' has tried to show); Beethoven as a suspected prowler; Debussy (and doubtless many others) for debt, as was Wagner, who in addition offended the authorities by supporting the revolutions that swept Europe in 1848.

Numerous British musicians were imprisoned as conscientious objectors during both world wars, most notably Sir Michael Tippett, who was locked up in Wormwood Scrubs just as the light-music composer Ivor Novello (real name David Ivor Davies) was being released, handing over to Tippett the bandmaster's baton of the prisoners' orchestra (they produced a better class of convict in those days). Novello's imprisonment was sadly ironic: in the First World War he had composed that great patriotic marching song 'Keep the Home Fires Burning'; but in the Second an unforgiving legal system put him in clink, not for conscientious objection but for fiddling petrol coupons.

Benjamin Britten took the easy way out and fled to the United States, conscientiously objecting from across the Atlantic, though he returned before the end of the war, at some risk to himself and Peter Pears. Britten's admitted habit of 'kissing and cuddling' the boy singers he loved working with would today have landed him in trouble for child abuse, especially at a time when homosexual relations even between consenting adults put many musicians into conflict with the law, until they were legalized in Britain in the 1960s. Russian laws were particularly draconian, and Tchaikovsky fell victim to them. He was freely able to have small boys living with him as 'servants', but when he started a relationship with the nephew of a tsarist official he was put on 'trial' by a kangaroo court convened by former fellow students.

The conductor and composer Eugene Goossens was convicted of importing 'obscene' material into Australia and forced to resign the directorship of the New South Wales Conservatoire. The stuff he carried was probably nothing that a European customs officer would have objected to, and would today be hardly noticed; but antipodean prudery knows no bounds (yet strangely does not extend to four-letter words, some of which are recognized as Parliamentary expressions).

Sir Thomas Beecham, whom today's press would inevitably have

GO ON, ALF, PLAY SOMETHING IMPRESSIVE, LIKE AN ORATORIO.

(By kind permission of *Punch*)

1933

described as 'flamboyant', got into several scrapes. He was briefly in danger of arrest as a bigamist, having married the pianist Betty Humby in the United States in an inadequate ceremony before properly divorcing the first Lady Beecham (or rather, she divorced him, 'on grounds of extreme cruelty'). Beecham's attorney was quoted in the *New York Times* of 8 September 1944 as saying '... to assure compliance with the technicalities of English law it was advisable that a second marriage ceremony be performed at this time'.* In 1911 Beecham was cited in an American divorce suit brought by George Sherwood Foster, with whose wife he had had an affair. It must have irked him to be described in US papers not as 'the famous conductor' but headlined 'Pillmaker's Son Named'. July 1925 saw Beecham starring in another divorce court, this time in London, when 'another woman' was cited; and in April 1930 Westminster Magistrates Court issued a warrant for his arrest in connection with an unpaid £16 hotel bill. Sir Thomas's counsel pleaded that his client was such a busy man that he had put the bill in his pocket and forgotten about it. Instead of being jailed, Beecham was fined £10; but less than nine months later he was in trouble again, over debts of hundreds of thousands of pounds – squandered not on women but operatic ventures that failed.

Otto Klemperer had at least two brushes with American cops. Once the car in which he was travelling was involved in some minor collision in a mid-western town, and the resulting road-rage argument brought the police to the scene. Klemperer, nervous because he had a woman with him who was not his wife (they had been staying in hotels as man and wife, which was illegal in some states), lost his head and pointed a water pistol at the officer, who put him in jail to cool off. In today's American criminal climate he would probably have been shot dead on the spot.

---

*After Beecham married Betty Humby he could be rather unkind to her, too. After a disastrous performance by her of the Delius Piano Concerto under his baton, he was asked by a stagehand, while briefly offstage taking a curtain call, 'Shall we take the piano off the stage now, Sir Thomas?' To which Beecham replied, 'Just leave the bloody thing. It'll slink off by itself.'

Women also landed Klemperer in jail in New York, after one of his habitual visits to a red-light district, for he was a compulsive patron of whores. The conductor Walter Weller told Peter Spaull that when he, Weller, was leader of the Vienna Philharmonic, Klemperer failed to turn up at the hall when a concert was imminent. A search party was sent out and discovered him in a nearby brothel, disputing a prostitute's fees (which shows how important it is for an artist to employ a concert agent).

The great violinist Eugène Ysaÿe (1858-1931) was convicted in 1908 of striking a railway guard – something many frustrated passengers must have been tempted to do over the years – but he was merely affronted by the Belgian railway servant's attitude to him, the great artist, so he boxed his ears. The guard claimed that this had made him deaf, and Ysaÿe was ordered to pay him £320 in damages. However (as reported in *The Musical News* of 18 July 1908), 'Ysaÿe succeeded on appeal in getting the sum reduced to £60 on the grounds that the guard's hearing was already impaired before the assault was committed.' In the same year Ysaÿe himself became the victim of a crime, in Russia, when his precious 'Hercules' Stradivarius was stolen from his dressing-room. He never saw it again: it was recovered 16 years after his death.

At about the same time as Ysaÿe's brush with the railway guard, another violinist got himself into highly embarrassing trouble: the Czech Jan Kubelik (1880-1940), father of the now better-known conductor Rafael Kubelik, was involved in a court case which revealed what he would have preferred to keep from his public, namely that he had hired a publicity agent to get him a favourable press – with the aid of 'human stories' to publicize Kubelik's alleged good works. *The Musical Times* reported with some glee that Kubelik had engaged an advertising agent 'to keep his name prominently before the public, to which end he [the publicity agent] had arranged that the violinist should very publicly befriend a poor boy of 13 who was nobly playing on the streets of London on a three-shilling violin to support his mother'. Kubelik doubtless felt that the agent had not succeeded, and he refused to pay him, whereupon the agent sued and spilled the beans. The court found against Kubelik and obliged him to pay the agent £150 plus costs.

This kind of contrived public-relations exercise is nothing new in the late 1990s, when publicity-seeking royal divorcees use sick children as props for photo opportunities to gain them public sympathy; and young female violinists are packaged in translucent frocks and sold like condoms. But Kubelik's case was heard in 1912, when the world was comparatively innocent of such tricks, and was suitably affronted.

If pop entertainers qualified for inclusion in this book it would be a veritable 'Who's Who Who's Been in Jail' for drugs offences and, at the even seedier end of that trade, for crimes of violence, too.

Better draw a veil over what that great pianist Claudio Arrau (1903-91) was alleged to have done with some boys in a park in Australia. He would have 'strenuously' denied it, but his concert tour was abruptly terminated on the usual grounds of 'ill health', which in a sense it might have been.

At least two great composers turned to murder. In 1590 Carlo Gesualdo, prince of Venosa (c 1561-1613) killed his wife and her lover, possibly also their child, believing it to be the lover's. The full story, containing elements of homosexuality, flagellation and transvestism, is supported by contemporary court reports and may be read in my *Wives and Loves of the Great Composers*. The same goes for Alessandro Stradella (1644-82), a notorious seducer of his female pupils, who were all members of the nobility, which made him a target of vendettas by her male relatives. During the resulting skirmishes he killed some of them, but was finally murdered himself in dramatic circumstances.

Giacomo Puccini (1858-1924) was involved only as an unwilling accessory after the fact, by trying to protect his wife. The story of her jealousy (for which he constantly gave her good cause), which directly led to their servant girl's suicide, would have made a plot for one of his operas. Doria Manfredi was a simple village girl who devotedly nursed him back to health after a motor accident. Elvira Puccini, who was constantly spying on him – he called her 'the policeman' – once saw them speaking quietly together, and accused him of having an affair with the teenage girl. From that moment on, Elvira persecuted the child, attacked her physically and threatened to take her to the lake and drown her, then spread false rumours round the village that she was a whore. She made her life such a misery that the girl took poison and died a horrible, lingering death. An autopsy established that she was a virgin, so for once Giacomo had not been guilty. Elvira Puccini was prosecuted and obliged to flee, helped by Giacomo. Eventually the Puccinis compensated the poor parents with some paltry sum and Elvira escaped justice.

Carmen subduces Don José

In 1966 Ben Trovato, that inveterate finder and purveyor of musical blunders, sent me a page from *Punch* containing an article by Richard Huggett. It was based on the printed programme of a gala performance of *Carmen* which the author had attended earlier that summer at the Paris Opéra. He quotes extensively from the notes explaining the plot of the work, under the same headline as given above:

> Act I: Carmen is a cigar-makeress from a tabago factory who loves with Don José of the mounting guard. Carmen takes a flower from her corsets and lances it to Don José (duet: 'Talk to me of my mother'). There is a noise inside the tabago factory and the revolting cigar-makeresses bursts into the stage. Carmen is arrested and Don José is ordered to mounting guard her but Carmen subduces him and he lets her escape.

> Act II: The Tavern. Carmen, Frasquita, Mercedes, Zuniga, Morales. Carmen's aria 'The Sistrums are tinkling'. Enter Escamillio, a balls-fighter. Enter two smugglers (duet: 'We have in mind a business') but Carmen refuses to penetrate because

Don José has liberated from prison. He just now arrives (aria: 'Slop, here who comes!') but hear are the bugles singing his retreat. Don José will leave and draws his sword. Called by Carmen shrieks the two smuglers interfere with her but Don José is bound to dessert, he will follow into them (final chorus: 'Opening sky wandering life').

Act III: A rocky landscape. The smuglers sheller. Frasquita, Mercedes and Carmen draw the fortunes out of cards (so called 'triocards'). Carmen sees into her game a sign of death. Micaela come to meet Don José (song: 'I say that nothing frightens me'). Carmen's arrival breaks it off. Escamillo makes a date with Carmen for the next balls-fights. Don José leaves with Escamillo.

Act IV: A place in Seville. Procession of balls-fighters, the roaring of the balls heard in the arena. Escamillo enters (aria and chorus: Toreador, toreador, all hail the balls of a toreador. Enter Don José (aria: I do not threaten, I besooch you') but Carmen repels him wants to join with Escamillo now chaired by the crowd. Don José stabbs her (aria: 'Oh rupture, rupture, you may arrest me I did kill der). Oh my beautiful Carmen, my subductive Carmen ...

So far so good. But a little later that year Ben Trovato sent me a cutting from the *New Yorker*, in which was printed a *Carmen* synopsis not very different from the above, but with appreciable differences. This time the anonymous writer claimed he had bought it at a performance in Genoa, Italy.

Was somebody making it all up, embellishing as he went along? Maybe, but the mystery deepened still further. For a little while later I bought an actual, lavishly colour-printed programme bound with a silken, tasselled cord, issued for a Gala Performance of *Carmen* at the Paris Opéra, on the occasion of the *XVIIIe Congres Mondial Vétérinaire Soirée du Juillet* 1967. The programme is dated 21 July 1967, that is, nearly a year *later* than the *Punch* article and a little after the *New Yorker* cutting.

Again there were considerable differences – certainly some improvements in the English – but with other mistakes added. Truly, Ben Trovato works in mysterious ways.

RATHER A LARGE ORDER

Mrs P de T: WELL, GOODBYE, DEAR DUCHESS! OH, BY THE WAY, MAY I BRING VON HUMM TO YOU TOMORROW NIGHT? HE'S A GREAT ORGANIST, YOU KNOW.
Her Grace: BY ALL MEANS! AND TELL HIM TO BRING HIS INSTRUMENT WITH HIM.

(By kind permission of *Punch*)
1884

Sir Arthur Sullivan blunders – and is hoaxed

For a man who wrote the music for all those deliciously witty Savoy operas, Sullivan often displayed surprisingly little wit himself. His diary is tediously earnest, throwing little light on the momentous events he witnessed in the musical life of London and Paris, though it is alleviated by frequent references to the date, number and quality of his sexual encounters, as well as the identity of his partners. But if his much and variously occupied bed ever moved to the sound of laughter he gives no indication of it, only to the keeping of statistics concerning his sexual prowess. When he provided music for the 82-year-old Alfred Lord Tennyson's verse-play *The Foresters*, Sullivan apparently took in his stride lines like this absurd duet between the First fairy and Titania:

> Tit, my Queen, must it be so?
> Wherefore, wherefore should we go?
>
> I Titania, bid you flit,
> And you dare to call me Tit!

Indeed Sullivan unknowingly committed a bigger blunder when, for the sake of heightening local colour in *The Mikado*, he included the song 'Miya sama, miya sama', having been told it was a genuine Japanese ditty. So it was, but the words are said to be grossly obscene – 'the foulest song ever sung in the lowest tea-house in Japan.' Nevertheless, in England, they have been innocently sung thousands of times in village halls and schools all over the English-speaking world, wherever *The Mikado* is performed. Ian Bradley, in *The Annotated Gilbert and Sullivan*, wrote, 'I have myself been offered an obscene translation of this line ... which I feel compelled to withhold from the eyes of my gentle readers.'

Arthur Jacobs was unfortunately unable to throw any light in his Sullivan biography on the existence of an alleged travesty called *The Bugger's Opera*, a scandalous skit on *The Beggar's Opera* which Sullivan was believed to have written, possibly with W S Gilbert or else in collaboration with the humorist George Augustus Sala. Professor Jacobs suggested the possibility of a Sala connection because that journalist and wit was credited with the words for a *Sods' Opera*. Professor Jacobs also put forward the plausible idea that Sala's *Sods' Opera* might simply have been sung to well-known Sullivan tunes, with or without the composer's knowledge. I knew an old gentleman who claimed to have seen a score of the work in the 1920s and confirmed the names of several characters long current in guffawing hearsay among English gentlemen in English gentlemen's clubs. They include the heroine, Felicity F–ckwell and Scrotum, a Wrinkled Old Retainer.

WHAT NEXT?

Mistress (to new housemaid): JANE, I'M QUITE SURPRISED TO HEAR YOU CAN'T READ OR WRITE! I'M SURE THAT ONE OF MY DAUGHTERS WOULD GLADLY UNDERTAKE TO TEACH YOU …

Maid: OH, LOR', MUM, IF THE YOUNG LADIES WOULD BE SO KIND AS TO LEARN ME ANYTHING, I SHOULD SO LIKE TO PLAY THE PIANNER!

(By kind permission of *Punch*)
1872

MUSIC AT HOME

Mistress (who can't bear kitchen music): Isn't that cook, Mary, singing 'The Minstrel Boy'?

Maid: Yes, ma'am.

Mistress: I wish to goodness she'd leave off!

Maid: Yes, ma'am – so dreadful out of tune one can't join in, ma'am!

(By kind permission of *Punch*)

1874

Handy gardener wanted, willing musician preferred

At the turn of the last century a musician was obviously required to be a person of many parts, according to these press advertisements:

John Towill, Gardener to the Earl of Glasgow, and Vicar Choral (Bass) of the Cathedral of the Isles, Cumbrae, will shortly be disengaged. He possesses a baritone voice and is a good musician, competent to teach a choir or brass band if required.

The Musical Times, 1879

Wanted by Respectable Lady: Maid Companion who is a good dressmaker and can play the pianoforte.

The Times, 1921

Pianoforte/violinist is willing to Exchange high-class lessons (with orchestral experience if desired) for thoroughly good and up-to-date bicycle.

The Musical Times, 1903

A lady of title requires a strong young man over twenty years of age, as odd man, to carry coals all over a country house and sing tenor in the choir.

The Musical Times, 1894

Respectable Young Man desires to learn music for pianoforte in return for window-cleaning.

St John's Wood Advertiser, 1892

Wanted, a Coachman; a man having a tenor voice and fair knowledge of music, so as to be able to take his part in a choir. Also, a Boy, to milk and take charge of cows; he must have a good voice.

The Musical Times, 1857

Tonic sol-fa Journeymen tailors. Wanted, early in the Spring, a Journeyman Tailor qualified to teach Mrs Curwen's notation. The situation will be permanent, and, for a married man, a desirable one. Apply to George Brocklesby, Caistor, Lincolnshire.

The Musical Times, 1870

Epilogue

On running the contents of this book through a spell-check on my computer I discovered that many words and names were misprinted. This is how they should have appeared:

Arnold Schönberg *Moses und Aaron*	Arnold Schooner *Modes undo Aardvark*
Benjamin Britten *Death in Venice*	*Death in Vehicle*
Carl Stamitz	Call Stamina
Felix Mendelssohn Bartholdy	Feline Meddlesome Bastardy
George Frederic Handel	Gear Frenetic Handed
Gilbert and Sullivan	Giblet and Sultana
Giovanni Gabrieli	Gigantic Gamble
Gustav Mahler	Gutsy Nailer/Guitar Mauler
Harrison Birtwistle	Harridan Birthrate
Henry Purcell: *Dido and Aeneas*	Heady Purely: *Dildo and Aegis*
Johann Sebastian Bach	Buck or Back
Johann Sebastian Bach: *Wachet Auf*	Joan Sensation Back: *Wallet Auk*
Johannes Brahms	Johnnie Braces
John Dunstable	John Dutiable
Ludwig van Beethoven: 'Egmont'	Lucid van Beehive 'Eggnog'
Madame von Meck	Madam vow Muck
Richard Strauss	Richer Strafes
Richard Wagner	Richer Wager or Wangler
Roland de Lassus	Road den Lasses
Romeo and Juliet	*Rodeo and Julies*
Siegfried's *Rhein Fahrt*	Siegfried's *Rhino Fart*
Sir Edward Elgar	Sir Edward Elgin
Thomas Tallis: *Spem in alium*	Themes Tallies: *Spam in Album*
Till Eulenspiegels Lustic Streiche	*Till Eucalyptuses lustier Stretch*
Tristan und Isolde	*Trepan undo Isle*
	Fruits Spiel